Access to History

General Editor: Keith Randell

Russia, Poland and the Ottoman Empire 1725–1800

Andrina Stiles

Hodder & Stoughton

LONDON SYDNEY AUCKLAND TORONTO

The cover illustration shows a portrait of King Augustus II of Poland, courtesy
The Nelson-Atkins Museum of Art, Kansas City, Missouri (Nelson Fund) 54–35

Other titles in the series:

The Ottoman Empire, 1450–1700   ISBN 0 7131 7827 2
Andrina Stiles

Europe and the Enlightened Despots   ISBN 0 340 53559 8
Walter Oppenheim

Russia, Poland and the Ukraine 1462–1725 ISBN 0 340 50784 5
Martyn Rady

France in Revolution   ISBN 0 340 51899 5
Duncan Townson

British Library Cataloguing in Publication Data
Stiles, Andrina
 Russia, Poland and the Ottoman Empire, 1725–1800. –
 (Access to history).
 I. Title II. Series
 947

 ISBN 0 340 53334 X

First published 1991

© 1991 Andrina Stiles

Typeset by Columns of Reading
Printed in Great Britain for the educational publishing
division of Hodder and Stoughton Ltd, Mill Road, Dunton Green,
Sevenoaks, Kent by

Contents

CHAPTER 1 Introduction   1

CHAPTER 2 Government and Society in the Early
           Eighteenth Century   5
           1 The Land   5
           2 The People   7
           3 Religion and the State   10
           4 Government   12
           5 Society   16
           Study Guides   22

CHAPTER 3 Russia 1725–63: Domestic Affairs   25
           1 Catherine I 1725–7   26
           2 Peter II 1727–30   26
           3 The Empress Anna and the 'Conditions'   27
           4 Ivan VI 1740–1   30
           5 The Empress Elizabeth 1741–61   31
           6 Peter III 1761–2   33
           Study Guides   39

CHAPTER 4 Russia, Poland and the Ottoman Empire
           1700–63: Foreign Affairs   41
           1 The Great Northern War   42
           2 The Russo-Ottoman War: The Pruth
              Campaign 1711   44
           3 The Ottoman War with Venice and Austria
              1714–17   46
           4 Persian Affairs   46
           5 The War of the Polish Succession 1733–8   48
           6 The Russo-Ottoman War 1736–9   49
           7 Diplomatic Developments   51
           8 The Seven Years War 1756–63   53
           9 Poland   53
           10 Overview   54
           Study Guides   55

CHAPTER 5 Diplomacy in the Eighteenth Century   56
           1 Diplomatic Organisation   56
           2 *Raison d'état*   61
           3 The Balance of Power   62
           4 Partition Diplomacy   63
           5 The 'Diplomatic Revolution'   65
           6 Diplomacy and the Enlightenment   66

              7   Conclusion   66
              Study Guides   67

CHAPTER 6   The Partitions of Poland: The First Partition
              1772–3   68
              1   Royal Election   68
              2   The Dissidents   72
              3   The Confederation of Bar   75
              4   Plans for Partition   76
              5   The First Partition   81
              6   Results of the First Partition   84
              Study Guides   87

CHAPTER 7   The Partitions of Poland: The Second and
              Third Partitions 1793 and 1795   89
              1   The Great *Sejm* 1788–92   89
              2   The War of the Second Partition 1792–3   94
              3   The Second Partition 1793   99
              4   The National Rising 1793–4   102
              5   The Third Partition 1795   107
              6   Aftermath   109
              Study Guides   110

CHAPTER 8   The Partitions of Poland: Reasons and Results   113
              1   Historical Views   113
              2   Poland's Internal Weakness   115
              3   The Greedy Neighbours   120
              4   Reasons and Responsibility   122
              5   Winners and Losers   122
              Study Guides   126

CHAPTER 9   Russia and the Ottoman Empire 1763–1800   131
              1   The Northern System   131
              2   The Russo-Ottoman War 1768–74   132
              3   The Treaty of Kuchuk-Kainardji 1774   135
              4   The Greek Project 1780–2   136
              5   The Crimea 1783–4   137
              6   The Russo-Ottoman War 1787–92   139
              7   Russian Dominance of Eastern Europe
                  – the Reasons?   141
              Study Guides   147

              Glossary   150
Further Reading   151
Sources on *Russia, Poland and the Ottoman Empire*   152
Index   154
Acknowledgements   154

Preface

To the general reader

Although the *Access to History* series has been designed with the needs of students studying the subject at higher examination levels very much in mind, it also has a great deal to offer the general reader. The main body of the text (i.e. ignoring the Study Guides at the ends of chapters) forms a readable and yet stimulating survey of a coherent topic as studied by historians. However each author's aim has not merely been to provide a clear explanation of what happened in the past (to interest and inform): it has also been assumed that most readers wish to be stimulated into thinking further about the topic and to form opinions of their own about the significance of the events that are described and discussed (to be challenged). Thus, although no prior knowledge of the topic is expected on the reader's part, she or he is treated as an intelligent and thinking person throughout. The author tends to share ideas and possibilities with the reader, rather than passing on numbers of so-called 'historical truths'.

To the student reader

There are many ways in which the series can be used by students studying History at a higher level. It will, therefore, be worth while thinking about your own study strategy before you start your work on this book. Obviously, your strategy will vary depending on the aim you have in mind, and the time for study that is available to you.

If, for example, you want to acquire a general overview of the topic in the shortest possible time, the following approach will probably be the most effective:

1. Read Chapter 1 and think about its contents.
2. Read the 'Making notes' section at the end of Chapter 2 and decide whether it is necessary for you to read this chapter.
3. If it is, read the chapter, stopping at each heading or * to note down the main points that have been made.
4. Repeat stage 2 (and stage 3 where appropriate) for all the other chapters.

If, however, your aim is to gain a thorough grasp of the topic, taking however much time is necessary to do so, you may benefit from carrying out the same procedure with each chapter, as follows:

1. Read the chapter as fast as you can, and preferably at one sitting.

2. Study the flow diagram at the end of the chapter, ensuring that you understand the general 'shape' of what you have just read.
3. Read the 'Making notes' section (and the 'Answering essay questions' section, if there is one) and decide what further work you need to do on the chapter. In particularly important sections of the book, this will involve reading the chapter a second time and stopping at each heading and * to think about (and to write a summary of) what you have just read.
4. Attempt the 'Source-based questions' section. It will sometimes be sufficient to think through your answers, but additional understanding will often be gained by forcing yourself to write them down.

When you have finished the main chapters of the book, study the 'Further reading' section and decide what additional reading (if any) you will do on the topic.

This book has been designed to help make your studies both enjoyable and successful. If you can think of ways in which this could have been done more effectively, please write to tell me. In the meantime, I hope that you will gain greatly from your study of History.

Keith Randell

CHAPTER 1

Introduction

Expansion, extinction, stagnation. These three words sum up the history of Russia, Poland and the Ottoman Empire respectively in the eighteenth century, shown in diagrammatic form below.

It needs only a quick glance at the two maps on page 2 to see how far-reaching were the territorial changes in eastern Europe during this period. These changes of frontier constitute one of the themes of this book: the expansion of Russia northwards at the expense of Sweden, westwards at the expense of Poland and southwards at the expense of the Ottoman Empire; the extinction of Poland, partitioned by her neighbours; and the stagnation, spiritual and material, of the Ottoman Empire, resulting in her decay.

However, even more important than the events themselves are the reasons why they happened. Why was Russia able to extend her frontiers so successfully? Why was Poland unable to resist aggression?

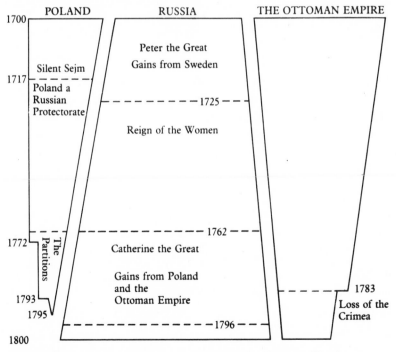

The relative strength of Russia, Poland and the Ottoman Empire 1700–1800

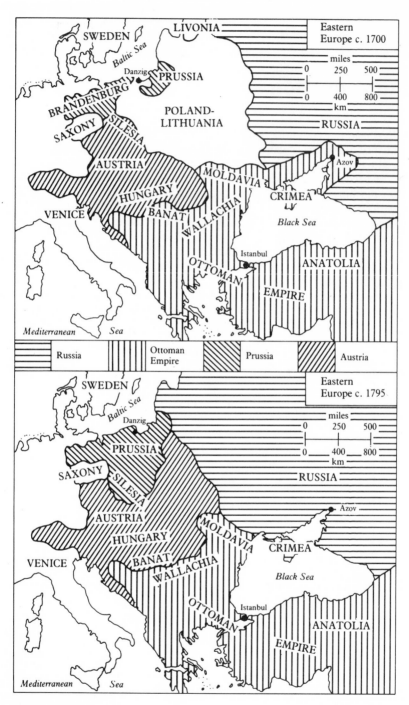

Eastern Europe

Why was the Ottoman Empire unable to change with the times? Answers based on primary source material as well as on the writings of British and foreign historians form the second theme of this book. Such answers cannot be definitive – the evidence is often inconclusive or contradictory, and historical opinion is divided. In the case of the partitions of Poland, for instance, was it Poland's own weakness or the strength of her neighbours which led to her destruction? Historians have been disagreeing over the answer for nearly two centuries because there is plenty of evidence to support both sides of the argument (see Chapter 8).

Set out in the flow chart on page 4 are some of the major issues, together with an indication as to where in the book they are discussed. The chart may at first appear complicated. It is not as difficult as it looks, but for the moment you will probably find it best simply to note that it is there. As you progress through the book, and the pieces of the jigsaw begin to fall into place, come back to the chart. It will repay careful study and provide a useful guide to revision of the topics dealt with in this book.

It is difficult to imagine three powers more apparently dissimilar from one another than were Russia, Poland and the Ottoman Empire in 1700. An understanding of their differences (as well as their occasional, unexpected similarities) helps to explain why their relations developed as they did in the course of the eighteenth century. The book, therefore, begins with a 'compare and contrast' survey of government and society in the three countries, from which you will be able to draw some conclusions for yourself about their relative strengths and weaknesses.

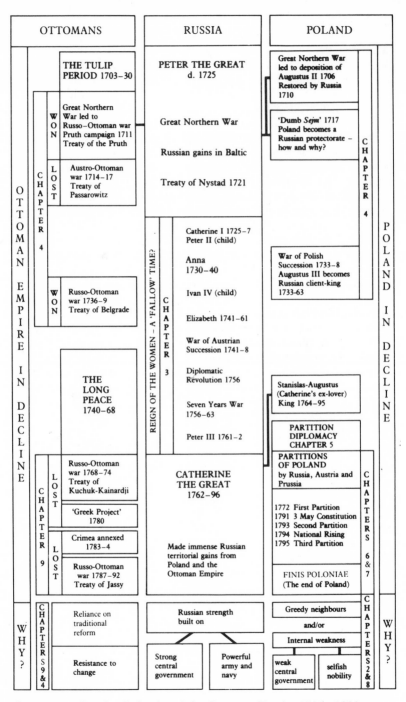

OTTOMANS			RUSSIA	POLAND	
		THE TULIP PERIOD 1703–30	PETER THE GREAT d. 1725	Great Northern War led to deposition of Augustus II 1706 Restored by Russia 1710	
O T T O M A N E M P I R E I N D E C L I N E	CHAPTER 4	WON — Great Northern War led to Russo–Ottoman war Pruth campaign 1711 Treaty of the Pruth	Great Northern War Russian gains in Baltic	'Dumb *Sejm*' 1717 Poland becomes a Russian protectorate – how and why?	CHAPTER 4
		LOST — Austro-Ottoman war 1714–17 Treaty of Passarowitz	Treaty of Nystad 1721		P O L A N D I N D E C L I N E
			REIGN OF THE WOMEN – A 'FALLOW' TIME?	Catherine I 1725–7 Peter II (child)	
		WON — Russo-Ottoman war 1736–9 Treaty of Belgrade	CHAPTER 3	Anna 1730–40	War of Polish Succession 1733–8 Augustus III becomes Russian client-king 1733-63
				Ivan IV (child)	
		THE LONG PEACE 1740–68		Elizabeth 1741–61	
				War of Austrian Succession 1741–8	
				Diplomatic Revolution 1756	Stanislas-Augustus (Catherine's ex-lover) King 1764–95
				Seven Years War 1756–63	
				Peter III 1761–2	PARTITION DIPLOMACY CHAPTER 5
	CHAPTER 9	LOST — Russo-Ottoman war 1768–74 Treaty of Kuchuk-Kainardji	CATHERINE THE GREAT 1762–96	PARTITIONS OF POLAND by Russia, Austria and Prussia	CHAPTERS 6 & 7
		'Greek Project' 1780		1772 First Partition 1791 3 May Constitution 1793 Second Partition 1794 National Rising 1795 Third Partition	
		LOST — Crimea annexed 1783–4 Russo-Ottoman war 1787–92 Treaty of Jassy	Made immense Russian territorial gains from Poland and the Ottoman Empire	FINIS POLONIAE (The end of Poland)	
WHY?	CHAPTERS 9 & 4	Reliance on traditional reform	Russian strength built on	Greedy neighbours	CHAPTERS 2 & 8
				and/or	
		Resistance to change	Strong central government / Powerful army and navy	Internal weakness	
				weak central government / selfish nobility	
					WHY?

Summary – Russia, Poland and the Ottoman Empire 1725–1800

CHAPTER 2

Government and Society in the Early Eighteenth Century

Government and society in early eighteenth-century Russia, Poland and the Ottoman Empire had some similarities; in other ways they were totally different from one another. Culturally and in matters of religion, too, there were marked differences, but also unexpected points of contact. By comparison and contrast each state is seen to have its own strengths and weaknesses.[1]

1 The Land

In the early eighteenth century the territories of all three powers were large. The Ottoman Empire stretched from the Danube in the north to the Nile in the south, from Algiers in the west to Baghdad and beyond in the east; it included territory in Europe, the Middle East and North Africa within its boundaries. Almost as large was Russia, bordered in Europe by Poland in the west, the Arctic in the north and the Black Sea in the south, and stretching eastwards beyond the Urals into Asia and the wastes of Siberia. Much the smallest of the three was Poland (properly, the Republic of Poland-Lithuania – see page 14). But this smallness was only comparative. Poland was for long the largest state in Europe, until overtaken in area by Muscovy in the mid-seventeenth century. Fifty years later, even after some loss of territory, Poland was still about the size of modern France and Spain combined.

Russia is an inherently poor country, whose inhabitants have always been hampered by its climate. Across the extreme north of the country lies the frozen and uninhabitable tundra; south of this is the great forest zone of conifers which changes to deciduous woodland as it meets the southernmost belt of vegetation – the grassland steppe. The fertile black earth of much of the steppe is the only part of Russia where arable farming is easy or productive. Its acquisition by Catherine II towards the end of the eighteenth century, as a result of her drive southwards to the Black Sea and her victory over the

[1] NOTE: Throughout this book, unless specifically stated otherwise, Russia should be taken to mean Russia west of the Urals; the Ottoman Empire to mean Anatolia, Ottoman lands between the Black Sea and the Caspian Sea, and most of the Balkans; and Poland to mean the Republic of Poland-Lithuania. (See the map on page 2.)

Ottomans, was of inestimable value to Russian agriculture. But even in these Black Lands, difficulties abounded.

The Russian climate is one of extremes, hot in summer and very cold in winter, particularly in the north and east. The problems created by these temperature variations are made worse by the uneven rainfall distribution, which can result in spring droughts and disastrous heavy downpours in late summer, making failed harvests common. One British historian has gone so far as to suggest that the decision of the earliest Slav settlers to rely on agriculture (rather than hunting, fishing or livestock breeding) in 'an area uniquely ill-suited for farming' and 'suffering from adverse natural conditions', was 'the single most basic cause of the problems underlying Russian history'. A similar theme is taken up by Russian historians. They see the climatic factor as the cause of the Russian's 'notorious aversion to sustained, disciplined work'. A great deal of work in the fields had to be done very quickly during the short summer. Eighteen hours a day was common, and around the clock not exceptional during harvest, with the peasant working his lord's fields by day and his own strips by night. Once the winter began, work became impossible. 'Thus, the Russian has accustomed himself to excessive short bursts of energy . . . No other nation in Europe is capable of such intense exertion over short periods . . . but nowhere else shall we find the same lack of habit for moderate and well distributed steady work . . .'. There was no margin of time available during the summer for agricultural experiments, which might prove unsuccessful. For if they were, the end result would be famine. Not surprisingly the Russian peasant preferred to stay with ways which he knew. This resistance to change remained a feature of the great mass of Russian society until modern times.

Neither the climate nor the agricultural problems are as severe in Poland as in neighbouring Russia. The temperatures are not as extreme nor the rainfall as capricious, and conditions are generally more favourable for farming, particularly in the south. During most of the life of the Republic the rich lands of the Polish Ukraine were available, and provided the basis for the important export trade in grain during the sixteenth and seventeenth centuries. In the earliest known account of Poland, written in the mid-eleventh century, the author states that the people there 'inhabited the richest limits of land suitable for settlement'. Certainly in Poland, unlike Muscovy, a peasant family was always able to produce enough food to support itself without difficulty in times of peace.

Much of the Balkans are extremely mountainous, and suitable only for grazing. In Ottoman times these areas were largely uninhabited except by nomadic shepherds and brigands. Along the coast and in the Danube and other river valleys conditions were more favourable for settlement and agriculture. Severe winters and wet summers seem to have hampered Ottoman military campaigns in the north all through the sixteenth century (to judge from the diaries kept by Suleiman the Magnificent) while in the south the problems were heat and drought. Anatolia (modern Turkey and the Ottoman homeland) is geographically and climatically diverse, ranging from the pleasant fertile coast lands through the barren centre to the high mountains of the east, where the Ottomans struggled through deep snow on many occasions whilst campaigning against the Persians.

2 The People

The Ottoman Empire, covering as it did such a large area, contained a wide diversity of races. The Turks (Turcomans), a nomadic people originating in the steppes of Asia, had migrated south and west into Anatolia in the twelfth century. A century later one of them, Osman, founder of the Ottoman dynasty, established an emirate (principality) on the north-western coast of Anatolia. In the course of the next 300 years his successors and their followers conquered the Balkans, the Crimea and the Caucasus, Syria, Egypt and North Africa, incorporating into their empire a great variety of peoples. Most of the small governing/military class of 'Ottomans' were not Turks – at least not until the late seventeenth century. They came from many areas but particularly from the Balkans (see page 16). The great majority of Turks were peasants who eked out a living in Anatolia, but some, especially in the early days of the Empire, were forcibly deported and resettled in the Balkans. There they lived alongside (and to some extent inter-married with) the existing, mainly Slav, populations. These native inhabitants themselves were often uprooted by the Ottoman government and sent to occupy underpopulated areas elsewhere in the Balkans. One result of all this movement was a complete confusion of nationalities within the Balkan peninsula. This was unimportant to the Ottomans whose political organisation took no account of differing nationalties within their empire. Only a man's occupation and his religion were of any signficance in establishing his position in Ottoman society – his racial origin was irrelevant.

   * Both Russia and Poland had populations which were mainly Slav in origin. The Slav peoples were nomadic tribes of cattle-grazers whose origins are obscure, but who are thought to have moved from Asia westwards into Europe, perhaps as early as the fourth century. After pausing in an area north of the Carpathians, they seem to have divided themselves into three main groups at some stage in the sixth or seventh centuries. One group moved north and east towards the Baltic and were the ancestors of the Russians (Ruthenes); a second

group turned south to colonise the Balkans and became the Serbs, Croats and Bulgars, while the third group continued west into central Europe, to establish themselves as the forbears of, among others, the Czechs, Slovaks and Poles. The Slavs of central Europe began early to refer to themselves as 'Slovianie' – the people with the gift of speech (as opposed to the 'dumb ones', their name for all their European neighbours, especially the Germans).

The Russian plain was settled by a branch of the eastern Slavs, who dispossessed the existing inhabitants. This vast region, which came to be known as Kiev (or Kievan) Rus – the Slav lands of Kiev – stretched north from that city to the Gulf of Finland. Made up of a number of principalities the state flourished until in the thirteenth century it fell to Mongol invaders from the south-east. During the two centuries of indirect Mongol rule which followed, one of the most insignificant of the dozen or more Slav principalities – Muscovy – slowly emerged to dominate all the others. This was largely because of its position on the Moscow River, where it was sheltered from attacks by Lithuanians from the north-west or by Tartars from the south and east. It was also well placed at the centre of north-south and east-west trade routes, and ideally positioned for political expansion. Muscovy took full advantage of all these facts. The aggressive policies of the Muscovite rulers from the fifteenth century onwards transformed Muscovy into Russia. The pretensions of Russia to be recognised as a major power at the start of the eighteenth century were symbolised by the claim of Peter the Great in 1721 to be Emperor of All the Russias. This claim proved a source of friction in the years which followed with, among others, the kings of Poland, who, as rulers of Lithuania, were Dukes of Rus.

Wielkopolska (or Great Poland) between the Oder and the Vistula rivers had been colonised by groups of western Slavs about the same time as the eastern Slavs were settling in Rus. These western Slavs came to be called 'Polanie' – the people of the open fields – which well describes the countryside of central Poland. To the east of the Vistula, along the Baltic shore, other groups settled. Among these were the Prussians and the Lithuanians. By the mid-fifteenth century the Lithuanians had expanded their territory to the south and east, and had established a large, independent Grand Duchy, stretching from the Baltic in the north to the Black Sea in the south. In doing this they took over part of the former Kiev Rus (or Ruthenian) lands. Under Lithuanian rule these areas still kept their old names – White Ruthenia (Byelorussia), the Ukraine, Red Ruthenia, Black Ruthenia – and the Old Ruthenian language. Even after the formal union with the Kingdom (Korona) of Poland in 1569, the Grand Duchy of Lithuania kept its own laws, treasury and army. Although it now shared a king and parliament (the *Sejm*) with Poland, Lithuania continued to be more Russian than Polish in character and outlook.

The dividing line between Russia and Lithuania was always an indistinct one. This was due not only to their shared ethnic and cultural heritage, and to the lack of any obvious geographical line of demarcation. It was also due to the fact that, even as late as the beginning of the eighteenth century, the modern idea of clearly defined frontiers, already established in the west, was not found in eastern Europe. In a region of great distances and sparse populations the pattern was one of small areas of settlement separated by large tracts of empty land – the Wild Plains of the Ukraine for instance. In such border areas the loyalties of the scattered communities wavered according to circumstances – in an emergency they turned to whoever was strong enough to offer the most protection, or against whoever was weak enough to provide opportunities for gain. Remote areas could, and did, change hands without occasioning comment from Moscow, St Petersburg, Wilno or Warsaw.

A great deal has been written about the geographical difficulties which have faced Poland – 'Poland's geography is the villain of her history'. Sitting in the North European plain, and with inadequate natural frontiers (so the argument goes), Poland has always been a natural prey to rapacious neighbours. Her territory has been invaded from all sides at frequent intervals, and been fought over or marched through by Germans, Russians, Austrians, Swedes, and Ottoman Turks. Yet it can be argued that Poland's position was no more exposed or dangerous than that of her immediate neighbours, Germany and Russia – her boundaries little different in geographical terms from theirs. Why then was Poland so vulnerable? The blurring of identities on the Lithuanian-Russian border may have been a contributory factor in making Russian involvement in Poland easier during the eighteenth century, but the answer to the question of why Russia and Prussia were able to devour Poland without serious difficulty is a political and not a geographical one (see page 68).

To the north of Poland on the shores of the Baltic were the Prussians, a people racially akin to the Lithuanians. In the early Middle Ages their small independent state of Prusy, or Borussia (Prussia), fought off all attempts at conquest by Poland or Lithuania. Eventually, tired of their marauding activities, a thirteenth-century Polish ruler took a decision which was to prove momentous. He invited the Military Order of Teutonic Knights to launch a crusade to conquer, for their own use, the still heathen Prussia. By slaughtering most of the native inhabitants and replacing them with German colonists, the Knights quickly turned Prussia into a German state. The western part of this state was eventually incorporated into Poland as Royal, or West Prussia, in the mid-fifteenth century, at last giving land-locked Poland access to the sea. The eastern part continued under the control of the Teutonic Knights until 1525, when, as Ducal or East Prussia, it became a Polish fief. Granted to the Elector of

Brandenburg and his heirs, it was ruled by the Hohenzollerns as one half of their state of Brandenburg-Prussia. In 1701 the Duke of Prussia proclaimed himself King *in* Prussia. Despite Polish protests, in 1725 he adopted the title King *of* Prussia. German East Prussia had become, *de facto* if not *de jure*, an independent state.

East Prussia, with its German-speaking inhabitants, was not the only non-Slav area within Poland-Lithuania. The Ukraine, wild and remote – *ot kraina*, the 'place on the edge' of the civilised world – had been fought over by Poland and Muscovy during the seventeenth century and had eventually been divided between them in 1667. It was occupied mainly by Cossacks, who were a law unto themselves and who bitterly resented the loss of the Ukraine's independence. Their origins are uncertain, but they probably originated as a breakaway Tartar group, into which were assimilated renegades of all sorts from Russia, Lithuania, the Ottoman Empire and elsewhere. To be a Cossack was more about following a way of life – the word 'Cossack' means a 'free soldier' – than about belonging to a specific ethnic group. Anyone who lived in the Ukraine could call himself a Cossack if he wished.

3 Religion and the State

The Turks had been converted to Islam in the eleventh century before they reached Anatolia. After the Ottoman conquest of Syria in the early sixteenth century the Moslem Holy Cities of Mecca and Medina came under the protection of the Ottoman sultan, giving him the title of Caliph and making him the most important Islamic ruler in the world. Religion was of paramount importance to the Ottomans, and observance of the *sheriat* (religious law) controlled their whole lives. As the *ulema* (the religious hierarchy) taught, 'The state is subordinate to religion. Political authority is nothing more than a means of applying the *sheriat* to life'.

The early Ottoman sultans had taken very seriously their duty as *ghazis* (warriors for the faith) to extend Moslem territory by a *Jihad* (Holy War) against non-Moslem countries. Religious fervour was the driving force of the early Ottoman Empire. So it is perhaps surprising that, in view of their devotion to Islam, the Ottomans did not persecute or forcibly convert their conquered non-Moslem subjects, but simply made them pay additional taxes. The majority of the sultan's subjects living within the whole empire were Moslems, either by birth or by conversion, but there were substantial minorities of Greek Orthodox Christians, Armenians, Jews and a number of other smaller groups, in the Balkans and elsewhere. These minority religions were organised into legally recognised communities called *millets*, whose members were allowed to live their lives according to their own religious customs and traditions, as long as these did not directly conflict with the wishes of the state. The Ottoman Empire was not only multi-racial, it was a tolerant multi-faith society.

* Poland-Lithuania, too, had been a religiously tolerant state. But, unlike the Ottoman Empire, this was no longer true in 1700. Poland had been converted to Christianity at the end of the tenth century, although much of Lithuania remained obstinately pagan until the end of the fourteenth century. At that date a dynastic marriage uniting the two countries imposed Christianity on Lithuania. Nearly half the Lithuanians, though, chose to adopt the Orthodox faith of their neighbour, Russia, in preference to the Catholicism of Poland. In the sixteenth century the Reformation brought Lutheranism to the the German-speaking cities of north and west Poland, while Calvinism became particularly firmly established in Lithuania. With this proliferation of faiths the possibility of religious civil war was a real danger. That it was averted was due to the general atmosphere of toleration which had always allowed Christians, Moslems and Jews – Poland had the largest Jewish population in Europe – to live peaceably together. An Act of 1573 had declared that 'albeit we differ in religion, we will keep peace between ourselves and we will not for the sake of our various faiths either shed blood or confiscate property . . . imprison or banish . . .'. Unfortunately, even while the Act was being promulgated, the Counter Reformation, although carried out by the Jesuits most peacefully, 'not by force, or with steel, but by virtuous example, teaching and persuasion', was already destroying the Polish tradition of religious toleration.

By the middle of the seventeenth century Catholicism was firmly re-established in Poland. The idea grew that to be Polish one must be Catholic; to be anything else was to be 'foreign', unpatriotic. Poland became one of the most fervently Catholic countries in Europe. The Act of 1573 was altered to 'graciously permit' minority worship within certain limitations: restrictions were placed on non-Catholics and their civil and political rights were reduced. Partly as a result of this policy, a number of Orthodox Christians decided to protect themselves by breaking away from their own Church and accepting the Pope as their spiritual leader, while retaining their own Slavonic liturgy and their married priests. These Uniates, as they were called, represented a compromise between Orthodoxy and Catholicism which was unaccep-table to the faithful of either Church. The Orthodox in particular regarded them as traitors, as a result of which they were considerably persecuted in the latter part of the eighteenth century, while the Catholics regarded them as second-class members of the Church. Religious tolerance had become a thing of the past.

When they adopted Christianity in the tenth century the rulers of Kiev Rus, who had close commercial ties with Constantinople, chose the Byzantine or Greek Orthodox form of the faith. After the fall of Constantinople to the Ottomans in 1453, the Church in Russia lost contact, not only with its head, the Greek Patriarch, but with the rest of the Christian world. It became nationalist and inward-looking, and this led eventually, in 1589, to the appointment of a Patriarch based in Moscow to head what was now known as the Russian Orthodox Church. During the seventeenth century internal disagreements on doctrine and ceremonial resulted in a major schism within the Church, leaving it too weak to resist state interference. In 1649 church administration was brought under state control, and made subject to a state department, the Monastery Bureau. Soon afterwards the Church Council weakly agreed to a declaration that the temporal power took precedence over the spiritual power (that is, that the state was superior to the Church). By 1700 the Church was powerless to prevent the sequestration of church revenues to provide for Peter the Great's war expenses. Soon afterwards the Patriarchate was abolished, and the Church became ever more secularised as a result of increasingly firm state control. Independent action by the clergy had become impossible. The power of the Church, moral and political, had been destroyed by the state. It could provide no opposition to Russian autocratic government.

4 Government

a) The Crown

The autocratic power of the Russian Tsars was well established by 1700. The Tsar, 'honoured like an earthly god', was almost totally unrestrained by any custom, law, institution or social group. No other European ruler enjoyed such freedom of action. Some historians argue that the origins of Russian despotism lie far back in the early history of Muscovy. They suggest that in order to survive in the days of the Mongol invasions, and to expand at the expense of neighbouring principalities later, it was essential for the rulers of Muscovy to be able to command unquestioning obedience from their people. Only such obedience could provide the Muscovite princes with the power they needed for success. Another suggestion is that these princes took as their model the unlimited authority which the Tartar khans possessed. Whether this was so or not, it is certainly true that the Orthodox Church was responsible for establishing as unquestionable the idea that the Tsar was a semi-sacred being. It is particularly ironic, in view of later events, that the clergy should have preached the divinely appointed authority of royal power in Russia. By doing so they brought about their own downfall, endowing the Tsar with unlimited power as the vice-regent of God, to do as he wished on earth. Successive Tsars echoed the words of their sixteenth-century predecessor, Ivan IV – 'I was born to rule, by the grace of God', and reaffirmed a belief in their personal God-given right to rule.

Authority in all spheres of life was concentrated in the Tsar – political, military, economic and religious – not only in theory, but also in practice. He was head of state, the sole political authority, commander of the army, owner of the land, ruler by divine right and controller of the Church.

* The Ottoman sultan also was an autocrat. In theory, but not in practice, his power was even more absolute than the Tsar's – over the land and over his subjects anywhere in the Empire. He was head of state, commander-in-chief of the army, head of government, chief justice and treasurer. He was also *imam*, head of the religious institution and controller of the whole body of religious personnel – teachers, judges, scribes and scholars. He could make laws – 'whatever the sultan decrees is law' – but only if they did not contravene the *sheriat* (the religious law). He could act in whatever way he pleased – but only as long as his actions conformed with the teachings of the *sheriat*. The constraints which the *sheriat* placed on the sultan made him less than absolute. It was the sultan's willing acceptance that the authority of Islam overrode the authority of the state, with the resulting religious and moral restrictions on his own secular power, which distinguished the Ottoman autocrat from that of Russia.

As with all autocracies, the maintenance of authority depended on the character and ability of the ruler. The seventeenth century had seen a marked decline in the personal qualities of the sultans compared with earlier times. This was due largely to the manner of the succession. Primogeniture had been introduced during the seventeenth century, but in order to ensure that there would be no rebellions or palace revolutions, all royal princes were kept shut in a special part of the royal palace, called the cage. There they might remain in captivity for the rest of their lives unless called upon, in order of age, to succeed to the throne. By the time they reached that stage, they were often mental and physical wrecks. This continued to be the situation during the eighteenth century, when most of the sultans were of low calibre (although there were some exceptions, notably Selim III). As a result, the central power of the Empire passed into the hands of officials and provincial 'notables', leaving the sultan more and more as a figurehead. Unlike Russia, which was not to reach its apogee of absolutism until the late eighteenth century, the Ottoman Empire presents a picture of steady decline in the sultan's exercise of absolute power by that time.

In the Ottoman Empire and in Russia there was, to a greater or lesser extent, a hereditary element in the choice of ruler. The Ottoman sultans all reached the throne in an unbroken line of descent from their founder Osman, and in fact continued to do so until the end of the Empire in 1923. In Russia the hereditary principle was established, although not always observed, until the situation was somewhat changed by Peter the Great. He abolished the law of primogeniture, a decision which gave rise to series of disputed successions and the creation of an increasingly non-hereditary monarchy during the eighteenth century (see Chapter 3). In Poland the situation was different. Indeed, the whole Polish system of government was totally unlike anything else in Europe. Its supporters believed it to embody a 'Golden Freedom', while its detractors described it as 'licensed anarchy'.

  * When Poland and Lithuania formally united in 1569 they became 'the Most Serene Commonwealth of the Two Nations', '*Serenissima Respublica Poloniae*'. Despite the title 'Republic', Poland-Lithuania was a monarchy. The Poles tried hard to explain this paradox by claiming that they had taken the best from both forms of government, making the Polish system the finest in the world. It was a republic because the enfranchised 'noble people' (the ten per cent of the population who counted as 'citizens'), chose their leader democratically; and it was a monarchy because the leader they chose was invested with the title, although little of the power, of a king. Every nobleman was entitled to vote at a royal election. Usually about 15,000 did so – all on horseback. They assembled on the Wola Field outside Warsaw to meet the candidates of which there were usually several, for any Catholic, whether Polish or foreign born, was eligible to stand for election. Sometimes, after a day of vigorous canvassing by the sponsors of the various candidates, a consensus of opinion led to the peaceful acclamation of one of the contenders as king. More often this did not happen, and fighting broke out on the field between rival groups – it was a dull election when, as in 1764, only 13 electors were killed. On a number of occasions the conflict could not be resolved on the Field at all, and spilled over into civil war conducted by two or more of the 'successful' kings-elect. The opportunities for foreign interference in an election were almost unlimited, and various combinations of French, Russian, Saxon, Swedish and Prussian financial and military resources were used to influence the outcome in 1697, 1717, 1733 and 1764. The dangers to the Republic's political independence and territorial integrity resulting from these 'free' elections are obvious, but were accepted by the *szlachta* (the nobility) as unimportant compared with the preservation of their individual right to vote.

Once elected, the new king's troubles were not over. He had to swear to accept certain restrictions on his freedom of action before his election could be confirmed. These restrictions were contained in an agreement called the *Pacta Conventa*. They included the king's recognition of the nobility's right to hold 'free' royal elections in the future, thus thwarting any dynastic plans which the king might entertain for his own family, and the nobility's right to approve taxes, declarations of war, and the summoning of the *levée-en-masse* (the whole nation at arms). In addition, the king was bound to summon the *Sejm* (parliament) regularly, and, most important of all from the nobility's point of view, was forced to recognise the *szlachta*'s right to band together in a legal armed Confederation. This allowed them to oppose, or, if necessary, depose the king if, in their opinion, he broke faith with them. This 'right of resistance' was the Polish nobility's treasured 'Golden Freedom', 'the inestimable diamond in the Polish crown'. While in Russia the eighteenth century saw the monarchy becoming increasingly elective, the absolute nature of sovereignty was never seriously questioned (not even in 1730 – see page 27). In Poland a royal election was merely the first step in restricting and controlling the king's freedom of action.

b) Representative Bodies

The Polish *Sejm* was a legislative body which normally met every two years for a six-week session. The senior clergy and officers of state made up the upper house of senators. From among their members 16 were appointed as resident advisers to the king, to accompany him and to supervise his actions wherever he might be. The lower house consisted of nearly 200 noble deputies, who acted in accordance with the instructions of the local *sejmiks* (meetings of nobles) which elected them. The principle had been established since 1652 that voting in the *Sejm* must be unanimous. No proposal could become law if a single dissenting voice cried out 'veto' (I deny), or '*Nie Pozwalam*' (I do not allow it). Not only was the proposal under discussion immediately abandoned, but the whole legislative programme already agreed in that session was rendered null and void. In such circumstances, the *Sejm* had been 'exploded', in the contemporary phrase, and the deputies immediately went home, with nothing achieved. By the eighteenth century the use of this *liberum veto* (the right of veto) had become excessive. During the entire reign of Augustus II (1733–66), for instance, only one *Sejm* was able to pass any legislation – all the rest were 'exploded'. Although the king could issue edicts, government action was severely hampered by these 'explosions', particularly where financial matters and foreign affairs were concerned, for there the king's power to act alone without the *Sejm* to ratify decisions was limited. There were obvious opportunities for foreign interference here, too. It was easy enough to find some impoverished backwoods deputy who could be induced by a large bribe to utter the necessary 'veto!' in order to prevent the passing of unwanted measures. The *liberum veto* was too useful to lose, and from 1717 onwards Russia in particular took great care to maintain it and to make use of it for her own purposes (see page 75). The weakness of the whole Polish parliamentary system was carefully nurtured by the Republic's enemies. From the mid-seventeenth century there were few treaties made by Russia, Austria, Sweden or Prussia which did not contain a clause referring to 'the necessity of defending Polish freedoms'. This meant 'stop the Poles from abolishing the veto'.

There was no representative body in Russia similar to the *Sejm*. Even the *Zemsky Sobor*, the so-called 'Assembly of the Land' which met for the last time in 1653, was never a representative body in the western sense of an Estates General. The *Duma*, or Council, made up of boyar (noble) representatives, acted as an advisory body to the Tsar, until it too became moribund in the seventeenth century. The nine-member Senate created by Peter the Great in 1711 merely transmitted the Tsar's orders and could neither initiate legislation nor fulfil any judicial function. Its members and those of its successor councils who were not elected, but were merely nominated by the monarch, had no independent authority.

There was nothing comparable to the *Sejm* in the Ottoman Empire either. There never had been. The *Divan*, the Imperial Council, which acted as an advisory body to the sultan and carried out his instructions, was made up of senior officials and members of the *ulema*. As the government's most important work was the administration of justice, this was the main function of the Imperial Council. It also discussed and took action on government business, but was not in any sense a legislative body. All secular laws, *kanuni*, were made by the sultan, or at least on his orders and were issued in his name. Long before the eighteenth century, the *Divan* had come to be presided over, not by the sultan in person, but by the Grand Vezir, the chief minister of the Empire and the sultan's deputy.

5 Society

a) The Nobility

Until the late seventeenth century the Grand Vezir and all other members of the Ottoman ruling/military class (the *askeri*) were slaves. A tax in the form of boys, the *devshirme* (the gathering), levied on Christian families in the Ottoman-held Balkans supplied most of the slaves needed. After collection they were taken to Istanbul, converted to Islam and divided according to ability. The best would enter the palace service as pages, from which they would eventually graduate to fill important posts in central or local government. These were the élite, highly educated men who formed the backbone of the Empire's administrative system, giving it a civil service more efficient than any in western Europe. The remainder of the boys would, after suitable training, become Janissaries, the formidable Ottoman infantry, or *sipahis*, the sultan's cavalry bodyguard. They too were slaves. There was no stigma attached to being the sultan's slave. It was the road to power and wealth. There was no aristocracy, no hereditary nobility of a western kind in the Ottoman Empire. Instead the slaves formed a meritocracy,

1 for the Turks do not measure people by any other rule than that of personal merit . . . no distinction is paid to birth . . . it is by merit that men rise in the service . . . they do not believe that high qualities are hereditary . . . therefore honours and high
5 posts are the rewards of great ability and good service . . . . all magnates and princes are officials made by the sultan and not lords or possessors.

Because it was solely their function in the state which determined their position in society, the *askeri* were akin to a service nobility of the kind introduced into Russia by Peter the Great. However, there were important differences. Because they were slaves, the possessions and wealth they acquired during their time in office reverted to the Sultan at their death – there was no hereditary element, and no land ownership, even among *timar* holders. These were the provincial *sipahis* (cavalrymen) who, as well as providing military service when required, also acted as local government officials. In return for these duties, they enjoyed the revenues from a certain area of land, but did not own the land itself. This remained the property of the sultan. There was in the Empire no system of feudalism of the kind found throughout Europe in the Middle Ages. Together with the Moslem-born members of the Learned Institution (the religious hierarchy of judges, teachers, scholars and scribes), the sultan's slaves of the Ruling/Military Institution formed the Ottoman class at the top of the social pyramid.

As the seventeenth century drew to a close the situation changed. It became uneconomic to continue collecting and training Christian boys from the Balkans for the sultan's service. Increasingly, free-born Moslems were admitted as pages, trained as Janissaries and given *timars*. This had been avoided before, because the slaves' total dependence on the will of the sultan ensured their loyalty, and Moslems could not, according to the *sheriat*, be made into slaves. As had been feared, self-interest to a large extent replaced dedicated service by the end of the seventeenth century. Bribery and corruption, always a problem in the Empire, increased, and there was a lowering of quality of the staff within the bureaucracy. At the same time, as central control weakened due to a series of incompetent sultans, the hierarchy of local administration collapsed. This was largely because of a breakdown in the *timar* system. The Janissaries had always been difficult to control. They now became completely out of hand, defied the sultan and took over large areas of the more remote provinces. There they married into local families, set up in business and grew rich, largely by oppressing the peasants. In 1700 the real power of the

Empire was passing into the hands of the Janissaries or those of the 'notables' or local war lords. In some areas the influence of both these groups was offset by that of the *ulema's* local network of *kadis* (judges) who took over much of the administrative work of former provincial officials.

   * In both Poland and Russia the nobility enjoyed a privileged status. The *szlachta*, or nobility, of Poland was one of the country's four largely autonomous 'estates'. The others were the Jews, the clergy and the burghers – the peasants, representing over 75 per cent of the population, hardly counted. The *szlachta* were not necessarily rich or landed. They were noble simply because at birth they had inherited nobility and all that went with it in the way of legal, fiscal and political privileges. They were exempt from taxation on the grounds that they had an obligation to provide unpaid military service when needed, although by 1700 this had very largely fallen into disuse, being no longer an effective method of raising a fighting force. Just at the time that in Russia the nobility were being burdened by Peter the Great with onerous service obligations, in Poland the *szlachta* had become a purely hereditary nobility with jealously guarded rights and no duties. The nobility controlled, entirely in their own individual interests, central government (through the *Sejm*), local government, and much of the economy. By the mid-eighteenth century anarchy, in its literal sense of 'no government', reigned supreme in Poland – the *szlachta* had made good their watchword '*Nierzadem Polska Stoi*' (it is by unrule that Poland stands).

   The great magnate families owned vast estates and uncountable wealth, maintained a 'noble retinue' or private army, made their own foreign alliances, monopolised the chief offices of state and fought each other as the mood took them. In the words of one modern historian, eighteenth-century political life in Poland 'was reduced to the feuds, follies and fortunes of a few families'. Below the magnates came the 'nobles with means', who possessed enough land to live on, and those (more than half the total nobility) with no land at all, who lived as peasants, worked as labourers and domestic servants or eked out a living as best they could in the towns. Some even sold themselves into serfdom; but all still remained noble, distinguished from their neighbours by the porches which they were entitled to build onto their hovels and on which they could paint a coat of arms. In addition they had the right to wear a sword, often a wooden one when they were too poor to own a steel one. These were the so-called 'nobles in clogs'. But, however impoverished he might be, a noble clung tenaciously to his 'Golden Freedoms'. The near-paranoid insistence of the nobility on maintaining the differential in status between themselves and the rest of society was only parallelled by their insistence on social equality within their own ranks – however obviously untrue this was in material terms.

There was an underlying reason for the difficulty which the *szlachta* had in coming to terms with reality. This was a romantic and deeply cherished belief, dating back to the sixteenth century, that they were all descended not from the same Slav ancestors as the peasantry, but from a superior warrior race, the Sarmatians, said to have migrated to southern Poland from the Black Sea regions sometime in the sixth century and to have conquered the docile Slavs whom they found there. Given that the *szlachta* were racially extremely mixed, consisting as they did of Poles, Lithuanians, Ruthenes, Germans and other Baltic peoples, as well as Tartars and Moldavians, there was no evidence for this belief. However, this did not disturb the *szlachta*'s sense of superiority, and by the seventeenth century they had created a whole way of life focused on all that was near-eastern, exotic and allegedly Sarmatian. Sarmatism was nourished by Polish contact with the Ottoman Balkans, and manners, clothes, furnishings and food were all influenced by Ottoman examples. The *szlachta* took to wearing Ottoman-style embroidered costume, admired Islamic art and design, copied Ottoman metalwork and followed Ottoman ideas of hospitality and display. In Polish hands this often became mere ostentation, for the *szlachta* did not like to put money away, but to invest in things they could exhibit – jewels, weapons, saddles and horses as well as clothes. By the eighteenth century Sarmatism as such was in decline, but it continued to form part of the noble ethos, which the *szlachta* believed set them apart from the rest of the population.

* The original Russian nobility, the *boyars*, with their great hereditary estates (*votchinas*), had been largely crushed by the mid-seventeenth century. In their place the Tsars had created a service nobility, the *dvoriane*. Their lands (*pomestyes*) were granted to them for life on condition of prescribed service to the state. By the time of Peter the Great the difference between the two forms of landholding was becoming blurred. Even the holders of *votchinas* served the Tsar; the *pomestyes* were no longer surrendered on the death of the holder, but were inherited by his family as long as service continued. A decree of 1714 recognised these facts, and established that all land was hereditable but was held only in return for lifelong service.

The whole life of a noble was therefore dominated by service and its demands, from his registration as a child to his final retirement or death. He received compulsory elementary education, without completing which, he could not marry. Even when he married, he had little chance of settling down or tending his estates. 'Noble families were often so scattered in the service that often one did not come into contact with one's relatives during one's whole lifetime'. At the age of 15 a young noble would either join a regiment or enter the bureaucracy to spend his life in peripatetic service, unless he could 'escape by judicious bribery, or by feigning illness or holy imbecility'.

As in Poland, there were wide differences in wealth and possessions among the nobility. Some new men like Menshikov (see page 26) made fortunes in state service. Others were so impoverished that they were only prevented by law from selling themselves into serfdom. Social niceties hardly existed outside St Petersburg or Moscow, even for old boyar families like the Golitsyns. When on their country estates they lived in manor houses little better than the houses of their serfs, except that they contained two rooms instead of one and had a larger number of icons.

In 1722 Peter the Great's 'Table of Ranks' made service to the state the basis of social status. The nobility spent the remainder of the eighteenth century attempting to free themselves from their onerous duties, and to form themselves into a closed, hereditary class. By 1763 they had obtained some concessions over the length of service demanded, but not over the principle of automatic ennoblement for anyone reaching a certain service rank. It was still true at the end of the century, as an English observer pointed out, that 'birth here gives but little claim to preference or consideration; both are regulated by the degree of rank acquired by service'.

b) The Peasants

At the bottom of the social pyramid in Russia, Poland and the Ottoman Empire were the peasants – more than three-quarters of the population in each case. In Russia and Poland life was hard, even for the small number of peasants who were personally free. For the majority, the unfree serfs, it was very hard indeed, and as the eighteenth century progressed it became harder.

Serfdom came late to Russia. Between the mid-sixteenth and mid-seventeenth centuries the majority of Russian peasants were enserfed in a gradual process aimed at preventing them from leaving the unproductive forest areas and migrating to the rich 'black lands' of the south. In an underpopulated country labour was in short supply. More 'hands' rather than more 'lands' brought wealth to the landowners, and a noble's income was computed according to the number of serfs or 'souls' he had available to work his estates and keep his house. Although serfs were not slaves – if they had been they would not have been liable to pay the poll-tax or to serve in the army, both activities essential to the functioning of the state – they came by 1707 to be regarded as the property of their lord. They owned neither house nor land, paid rent in money or kind, provided labour service three days a week, were bound to the land, were without rights and were entirely subject to the whims of their lord. Only the murder of a serf was not officially permitted to the owner.

By the mid-eighteenth century 'privately-owned' serfs (as opposed to church or state serfs) were coming to be regarded as attached to the person of their lord, rather than to a particular one of his estates. He could and did move them, with or without their families, to whichever part of his property needed additional labour. Whether they belonged to a noble landowner or to the monarch personally, such serfs could be given away – Catherine the Great presented 800,000 serfs as rewards to various recipients during her reign – or sold by auction or later through newspaper advertisements.

   * In Poland the *szlachta* preached brotherly love among themselves and charity and understanding towards other social groups. A nobleman's strength, it was said, lay in the love of his serfs. But from the seventeenth century onwards there was public condemnation of the over-work, the severe punishments, the torture and death sentences meted out to serfs by their lords:

1 God does not punish Poland for nothing
  But chiefly for the harsh oppression of the serfs
  Which is worse than slavery; as if the peasant
  Were not your neighbour, not even a person . . .
5 It is their hands which feed you;
  And still you treat them with such cruelty . . .

However, not all historians accept such a gloomy picture. Some believe that, although by 1700 the lord had come to have the power of life and death over his peasants, there was technically no serfdom in the Republic in the Russian sense. They assert that the peasant did not 'belong' to anyone, and was his master's subject only in respect of his contract to provide labour in return for his house and land. Nevertheless, the generally accepted view is that the sixteenth and seventeenth centuries saw a great extension of serfdom brought about by a boom in the Polish grain trade. The 'lord's right to unpaid labour services' had long existed, but the new demand for exported grain led landowners to exploit and regularise this casual arrangement. More work was demanded from the peasants, and their freedom to leave the estate was severely restricted. Gradually their legal and social rights were reduced as well. Matters were made worse by the severe agricultural recession in the early years of the eighteenth century, particularly in those areas ravaged by the Great Northern War. As a result of economic pressure, nearly all those peasants who were still free in 1700 found themselves reduced to the level of serfs by 1720.

   * The state of affairs in the Ottoman Empire was different, for there the peasants were, and always had been, personally free. The Moslem peasants, the 'Sultan's well-protected flock' (the *reaya*), and the non-Moslems (the *zimmis*) received equal treatment, apart from certain extra taxes imposed on the latter. As time passed, all became increasingly tied to the land, although they remained hereditary tenants of their house and land in the Balkans where the *timar* landholding system was still in force. However, peasants, especially in

Anatolia where conditions were less favourable, did run away to the towns or to the hills, especially in times of famine or civil unrest. Efforts were made everywhere to keep the peasants on the land, but if they did flee, no very serious attempt was made to recover them. If they did not return within a given time, usually three years, new occupants would simply be found for their houses and plots of land. Not until the end of the eighteenth century did the government order the forcible return of peasants to their home villages, whether or not there was anywhere for them to live or any work for them to do. Until then, the Ottoman government was, unlike its neighbours, sufficiently pragmatic in its approach to the peasant population to realise that there was nothing to be gained from excessive harshness. It was a matter of economics, and of state security (particularly in the Balkans) to protect the peasants, who not only worked the land and produced the crops, but paid the taxes to support the army. In the circumstances, the peasants had to be the sultan's 'well-protected flock' in fact as well as in name.

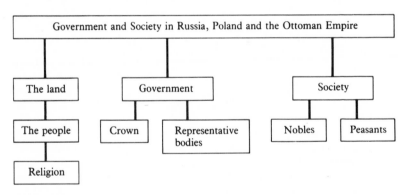

Summary – Government and Society in the Early Eighteenth Century

---

Making notes on *'Government and Society in the Early Eighteenth Century'*

This chapter contains background information on government and society in Russia, Poland and the Ottoman Empire in the years leading up to the beginning of the eighteenth century. While it is extremely unlikely that you would need the information as it stands in order to answer an examination question, it *is* important that you are aware of the similarities and differences between the three countries around 1700 and that you are able to draw some conclusions for yourself about the strengths and weaknesses of each at that time.

So rather than going through the chapter making straightforward notes on the three countries, it is suggested instead that under each of the headings used in the chapter you jot down, quite briefly:

a)   any points of similarity
b)   any points of difference
c)   any conclusions relating to relative strengths and weaknesses.

What overall conclusion, if any, do you reach? Is it possible to place the three countries in any sort of rank order? If so, what are the reasons for your choice of order?

Answering essay questions on 'Russia, Poland and the Ottoman Empire in the Eighteenth Century'

You are very unlikely to be faced with an essay question covering the whole scope of this book, but you might be asked to deal with a general question on *one* of three powers in the eighteenth century.

In the case of Russia it is most probable that such a question would be concerned with either the efforts of the nobility to obtain freedom from the service obligations imposed upon them by Peter the Great, or with changes in the nature of the monarchy. Examples are:

1.   'What were the most important changes in the status and functions of the Russian nobility during the eighteenth century?'
2.   'How successful was the challenge to autocracy in eighteenth century Russia?'

As only the period of Russian domestic history from 1725 to 1763 is covered in detail in this volume, you would need to use additional information from the companion volumes in this series in order to be able to answer the questions fully.

Any overall question on Poland will concentrate on Polish weakness during the eighteenth century:

3.   'Consider the causes of Polish weakness in the eighteenth century.'
4.   'Did Poland "present the spectacle of a country galloping towards its own destruction" in the eighteenth century?'

The overwhelming majority of questions set on Poland are concerned with the Partitions, and these are dealt with in detail at the end of Chapter 8.

The great days of the Ottoman Empire were past by the eighteenth century. During the period covered by this book the sultans sought vainly for acceptable ways to reform the Empire at home in order to be able to resist the enemy abroad. Occasionally a straightforward question may be asked about the Empire's domestic problems:

5. 'Did the Ottoman Empire alter in character during the eighteenth century?'
6. 'Why were the sultans unable to halt Ottoman decline during the eighteenth century?'

The Ottoman opposition to change goes far towards explaining *why* the Empire was incapable of successful resistance to Russian pressure during the reign of Catherine the Great. The Empire is often included as one of Russia's 'weak neighbours' in questions on Catherine the Great's foreign policy, and questions of this kind are dealt with at the end of Chapter 9.

CHAPTER 3

Russia 1725–63: Domestic Affairs

The period of Russian history between 1725 (the death of Peter the Great) and 1762 (the *coup d'état* which brought Catherine II to the throne) is largely ignored by historians as unimportant and unproductive – simply a time of palace revolutions which provided a succession of unimpressive rulers (two of them children), during whose reigns little was achieved. Is this a fair and accurate representation of the situation?

The constitutional and social history of Russia during the first half of the eighteenth century is made up of several connected elements. Continual struggles for the succession weakened the authority of the crown, which became increasingly elective, and enabled the nobility to demand a reduction in the autocratic power of the sovereign as the price of their support. The nobles had two aims in their dealings with the crown – to loosen state control over themselves and their families, particularly in respect of the onerous duties of service laid upon them by Peter the Great, and to increase their own grip on the lives and property of their serfs.

In some senses this period *was* a mere interlude, an interregnum between the reigns of Peter the Great at one end of the century and of Catherine the Great at the other. It *was* the 'palmiest of palmy days' for the favourite, the intriguer, the conspirator and the assassin; but, as a result of the *coups d'état* and palace revolutions which they helped to bring about, the nature of Russian society was profoundly changed.

The British ambassador to St Petersburg does not seem to have been impressed with the general situation as it existed in Russia in 1741:

1 After all the pains which have been taken to bring this country
  into its present shape . . . I must confess that I can yet see it in
  no other light than as a rough model of something meant to be
  perfect hereafter, in which the several parts do neither fit nor
5 join, nor are well glued together.

Most of the difficulties in glueing the parts together arose from the lack of a clear law of succession.

The death of Peter the Great in 1725 left a political vacuum. The larger-than-life Tsar who had dominated Russia, ordered its affairs and dragooned its people for so many years, was not easy to replace. There was no direct heir – Alexis, Peter's son by his first marriage had died in prison during his father's lifetime, and there was no surviving son of the second marriage. In 1722, three years before his death,

Peter abolished the succession law based on primogeniture and issued a decree giving him, and his successors, the right to nominate the heir. But he left his nomination too late. On his death-bed, unable to speak, he wrote the tantalising words 'Give all . . .', but to whom, he did not survive long enough to explain. This left the succession wide open. The contenders were: Peter's second wife, Catherine; Alexis's son, Peter (although he had been specifically excluded from the succession at the time of his father's trial); Anna and Elizabeth, the daughters of Peter the Great, and Catherine and Anna, the daughters of Ivan V (see the family tree, page 153).

1 Catherine I 1725–7

The choice fell on Peter's widow, Catherine, a Lithuanian peasant woman of limited intelligence, with no interest in anything except men, food and drink. She was proclaimed Empress by the Senate, after demonstrations by the Guards Regiments had been organised in her support by some of Peter the Great's friends. Among these was Catherine's erstwhile lover, Prince Menshikov, who 'from the lowest condition, was raised [by Peter the Great] to the highest station, and would have finished his career with honour if he had not been so infatuated with ambition'. He was the power behind the throne during the two short years of Catherine's reign. It was as the result of his advice that in 1726 she set up a Supreme State (or Privy) Council of seven members, headed by Menshikov himself, to rule on her behalf. This Council largely took over the work of the Senate created by Peter the Great.

There were very serious problems for the new government to deal with. There was a breakdown of law and order in the countryside, and outbreaks of violence, due largely to distress among the peasants brought about by heavy taxation, poor harvests and severe famine. Peter the Great had made the landowners responsible for seeing that the poll-tax was paid, but collecting it had become very difficult, and in many areas the peasants were unable to pay at all. Various changes were proposed but little was actually done to improve the situation.

2 Peter II 1727–30

As Catherine's health began to fail, she nominated Alexis's son, Peter, as her heir. As he was only twelve, she appointed the State Council as regent. A week after her death in May 1727, Menshikov took supreme control, proclaimed himself 'Generalissimus' and affianced his daughter to the new Tsar. A power struggle immediately broke out within the Council between the low-born Menshikov, who represented the 'new men', and members of the old, conservative boyar families of Golitsyn and Dolgurky. Menshikov was defeated and ousted from power. He was accused of misappropriating vast sums of money and land – he was almost certainly guilty – and exiled with his family to Siberia. But his real, if unspoken, crime in the eyes of his aristocratic enemies was his presumption in trying to place his descendants on the Russian throne.

For the remainder of his brief life the young Peter II was entirely under the influence of the Dolgurky family. As a result there was something of a return to the old ways, symbolised by the removal of the court from St Petersburg to Moscow. A series of decrees in 1727–8 tried to deal with the social and economic problems of the provinces by dismantling the whole local administrative system established by Peter the Great. It was replaced by a simpler organisation of provincial governors and local governors (*voevodas*). This eventually provided a more settled and peaceful provincial life, especially when later changes allowed more nobles to remain at home to administer their estates.

A Dolgurky daughter had been selected as a replacement bride for the Tsar, but on the day fixed for the wedding in January 1730, Peter died of smallpox, without naming a successor.

3 The Empress Anna and the 'Conditions'

This precipitated another succession crisis – the third in five years. The State Council, now dominated by Dolgurky and Golitsyn representatives, held an immediate meeting. Names were suggested and rejected. The choice was narrowed down to Ivan V's daughters, the second of whom, Anna, the widowed Duchess of Courland, appeared to be the most suitable. She was believed to be a compliant and obliging woman likely, as Empress, to do what she was told. In the eyes of those making the choice, this was an important point in her favour. So too was the fact that, as she was still only 35, a suitable remarriage might provide a direct heir for Russia. Her name was put forward at once, but the nomination was made subject to certain conditions. She must not remarry without the State Council's consent, nor name an heir. She must govern only through the Council, without whose permission she could neither declare war nor make peace, impose taxes, confer civil or military rank above that of colonel, grant titles or estates nor make use of state revenues. No noble was to be deprived of life, honour or property without a proper trial. Lastly, she must not bring her lover, Count Biron, with her.

Which member of the Council initiated these conditions is disputed. Some sources attribute them to Demetri Golitsyn, who had visited western Europe, had studied political theory and been much influenced by the ideas of constitutional monarchy which he found current in England and Sweden. He is reported to have addressed his fellow councillors on the merits of a limited monarchy:

1 Since by the death of Peter II the whole male line of Peter I is
extinct, and Russia has suffered extremely by despotic power, it
would be highly expedient to limit the supreme authority by
salutary laws, and not to confer the crown on the new Empress
5 but under certain conditions.

However, the Scot, James Keith, who was in Moscow at the time,
believed that the conditions were the work of the Dolgurkys, who

1 formed a scheme of government by which the Empress was to
have the name and they themselves the power . . . in a kind of
government half commonwealth, half monarchy and so ill
digested it was impracticable in any country, but much more in
5 Russia where the genius of the nation and the vast extent of the
empire, demands a Sovereign, and even an absolute one.

Negotiations with Anna led to her apparent acceptance of the
restrictions on her freedom of action, even though her authority was
further reduced by an oath forced upon the army, that it would serve
the Empress only in conjunction with the demands of the Council,
and would not give its allegiance to her alone. News of the
'Conditions' and Anna's agreement to them reached Moscow at the
beginning of February, where it caused some disquiet among the
nobles who had come to the capital for a wedding but instead had
attended a funeral and had then stayed on to find out who was to be
the Tsar's successor. Many gave their opinion that the Council had
been peremptory and heavy-handed in its management of the affair.
They considered that issuing conditions of this kind and in this way
was dangerous. It would transform Russian absolutism, not into a
limited monarchy, but into an oligarchy, from which only the
magnates, and not the great bulk of the nobility, would benefit. As
one of the lesser nobility expressed it:

1 God forbid that it turn out that instead of one autocratic sovereign we have tens of absolute and powerful families, and thus
we, the nobility, will decline completely and we will be forced
more painfully than before to make obeisance and to seek fav-
5 ours, and this will not be easy, for however much they are in
agreement now, there will soon undoubtedly be arguments
among them.

Views of this kind have led some historians to believe that the
lesser nobility (the *dvoriane*) had a clear preference for the continued
rule of one, rather than the rule of many, and that they were not
greatly concerned with restricting the absolute power of the sovereign,
as long as that power did not have an adverse effect on them

personally. Other historians do not agree. They see the events of 1730 not just as an attempt to introduce a limited monarchy and permit some effective power-sharing (if only by the magnates): they believe there was a much deeper and more significant constitutional crisis. The choice of sovereign by the Council, taken together with the imposition of conditions to be agreed before the accession could be confirmed, introduced an elective element into the monarchy. This was similar to that found in Poland (see page 14) and Sweden, with both of which Golitsyn was familiar. Yet other historians consider the events of 1730 to have little significance, 'a superficial change' of no lasting importance. Paul Dukes writes:

> 1 . . . the significance of the dramatic events of 1730 lay not in a
> bold attempt at constitutional reform nor in a craven acceptance
> of the system already in existence, but rather in an abrupt
> change of sovereign without much bloodshed or widespread
> 5 disturbance.

Once she arrived in Moscow, the Empress Anna 'took all pains imaginable to form a strong party', as a well-informed contemporary wrote:

> 1 She left no arts or managements unemployed towards effecting
> her purpose of creating misunderstandings among the members
> of the Council of State, and stirring up distrust of the Council
> among other members of the nobility. Everything succeeded to
> 5 her wish . . .

Several hundred of the lesser nobility paid a visit to the Empress, and their spokesman expressed to her the belief that she had been surprised and misled by the Council into making 'unreasonable concessions'. He concluded that 'Russia having been for so many ages governed by sovereign monarchs and not by council, the nobility begged her to take into her own hands the reins of government'. He added, for good measure, that the whole nation was of the same opinion. Anna then evinced well-simulated surprise. 'How? Was it not the will of the whole nation that I signed the act presented to me?' On receiving the expected, unanimous cry of 'No, no', she sent for the documents and herself tore them up, exclaiming,

> 1 The empire of Russia has never been governed but by one sole
> monarch. I claim the same prerogative as my ancestors, from
> whom I have derived the crown by right of inheritance, and not
> from election by the Council of State as they have pretended.
> 5 Whoever opposes my sovereignty shall be punished as guilty of
> high treason.

Anna was as good as her word. Autocracy was quickly reimposed. The Council was suppressed, and some of its members were arrested and executed or sent into exile. During the next few years 20,000 more of her subjects were sent by the Empress to colonise Siberia for taking part in alleged anti-government conspiracies. Some power was restored to the Senate, and a new body, the Cabinet, consisting of only two or three members became the chief organ of government. The court returned to St Petersburg, where the Empress did not concern herself greatly with government affairs. She preferred to leave them to her German friends and favourites headed by Count Biron, who had eventually followed her from Courland. His influence was believed, probably incorrectly, to be all-pervading, so that the whole reign is known in Russia as the *Bironovshchina*.

* The Empress had routed the Council of State with the support of the *dvoriane*, and of the Guards Regiments (composed largely of nobles) which had met and escorted her on her entry into Moscow at the start of her reign. Not surprisingly, therefore, the nobility expected a reward. They received it in the form of some relaxation of the state controls introduced by Peter the Great, and a return to earlier practice. At the end of 1730 the unpopular Entail Law of 1714 was abolished, leaving nobles free to divide their estates among all their heirs as they pleased. A year later the Noble Cadet Corps was established which enabled the sons of the nobility to proceed straight to commissioned rank in the army or bureaucracy without the unpleasantness of starting in the ranks. In 1736 the age at which compulsory state service began was raised from 15 to 20 and the period of service reduced from life to 25 years. By a further important concession where a family had several sons, one was freed from service altogether, so that he could look after the family estates.

A first step towards achieving the nobles' other ambition, greater control over the lives and property of their serfs, was taken in 1731, when nobles were entrusted with the actual collection of the poll-tax themselves. Five years later Anna issued a decree, similar to that of Peter the Great, authorising the punishment of any fugitive peasants 'by knout, whiplash or stick upon their apprehension . . . the nobles or their stewards to determine which punishment is appropriate'. In 1737 further restrictions were imposed, preventing a peasant from buying property except in the name of his lord. All these measures represented a further deterioration in peasant independence. Worse was to follow in succeeding reigns.

4 Ivan VI 1740–1

Anna was determined that her successor should be a descendant of her father, Ivan V, rather than of Peter the Great. This meant that only one candidate was available – her niece, Anna Leopoldovna. Biron had already tried to arrange a marriage between his son and this young woman, but his attempt had failed and she had married a minor German prince, the Duke of Brunswick. In August 1740, a son was born to the couple. Two months later the Empress died, having named the infant as her heir, with Biron as regent. Biron had not troubled during Anna's lifetime to ingratiate himself with the Guards or with high-ranking officials in the bureaucracy. Communication would in any case have been difficult for he never learned to speak more than a few words of Russian. Therefore the death of Anna found him with few friends and many enemies. A *coup d'état* was staged with the complicity of Anna Leopoldovna. The officer commanding the Guards detachment that carried out the *coup* left a long and detailed account of the events of the night. He described how Biron, woken from sleep, tried to hide under the bed, and how his wife was left lying in the snow outside the house by a soldier unwilling to carry her further. Biron (reunited with his wife) was exiled to Siberia and Anna Leopoldovna declared herself Regent for her son, Ivan VI, 'amidst great demonstrations of joy'.

Neither the joy nor the regency were to last long. In December 1741 yet another *coup d'état* brought Elizabeth, the daughter of Peter the Great and Catherine I, to the throne and Ivan VI (not yet two years old) to prison, there to spend the rest of his short life.

5 The Empress Elizabeth 1741–61

The good-looking, pleasure-loving Elizabeth had become an admired and popular figure with the nobles serving in the élite Guards Regiments during the 1730s. With their military backing, and with financial and diplomatic support from the French and Swedish ambassadors, she had begun to be a serious danger to the Regent by the end of 1741. So much so, that she was even threatened with being forced to enter a convent. For the worldly Elizabeth, with, as the British ambassador wrote, 'not one ounce of nun's flesh about her', this was an unthinkable future. Fearing immediate arrest, she put herself at the head of several hundred Guards in a march to the Winter Palace on a night in early December, 'to free Russia from our German tormentors'. Once at the Palace she rallied further support, allegedly crying to the soldiers, 'Wake up, my children and listen to me. You know who I am, and that the crown belongs to me as of right.' The Regent, the Tsar and his baby sister were arrested in what is reported to have been a touching scene, with Elizabeth kissing the children affectionately, before eventually sending the whole family off to prison. In the morning Elizabeth declared herself Colonel of the three Guards Regiments, issued a soothing manifesto explaining her acceptance of the throne as necessary to put an end to the confusions of the previous regime, and then appeared on the palace balcony to receive the plaudits of the people.

Historians in general have devoted more attention to the events of 1730 than to those of 1741, but there is one significant point about Elizabeth's accession. Although by 1741 the élite Guards Regiments had lost some of their earlier importance, they still retained an influence in state affairs, particularly in the making or unmaking of the sovereign (in which their role can be compared with that of the Janissaries in the Ottoman Empire). Between 1725 and 1796 almost all Russian rulers (Peter III was a notable exception) owed their accession to the active support of Guards officers and men; but increasingly this support was not enough on its own. It came to be effective only when combined with that of high-ranking civilian officials from the rapidly expanding bureaucracy. By the end of the century the civilians were taking over, and Elizabeth's accession *coup* is the last occasion on which the military involvement was all-important.

* The *coup* had been bloodless. Even the ex-Regent's advisers had their sentences commuted to exile at the last minute, to the disappointment of the crowd assembled to see them quartered or broken on the wheel. The unwillingness to shed blood was one of the abiding characteristics of Elizabeth as Empress; she is thought never to have signed a death warrant during her reign of 20 years, perhaps due to her deep and genuine piety. Described by some observers as charming, kind, majestic and lively, and 'worthy of admiration by all the world', she was also domineering, quick-tempered and, on occasion, vindictive. She was naturally indolent and she seldom exerted herself to any sustained action. Days were passed in idle gossip, hunting, banquets, dancing and festivities of all kinds. Her court became one of the most brilliant and immoral in Europe, and she herself the most extravagant of monarchs. 4000 of her dresses were destroyed in one of the many palace fires, but 15,000 more were found in her wardrobes after her death. The buildings in which she spent her time were, apart from the magnificent state rooms, mostly draughty, wooden constructions, dirty, leaking and verminous, but she and her courtiers were magnificent in silk and satin, festooned with jewels, their hair elaborately dressed and powdered. This stark contrast between the court and its surroundings was one of the first impressions recorded by the young German girl, later to be Catherine the Great, when she came to Russia in 1744 to wed Elizabeth's nephew and heir, Peter.

Elizabeth's reign is sometimes said to mark a rejection of the 'German yoke' in favour of a return to Russian ways. Whether this was an improvement is open to question, given the low intellectual ability of most of her advisers and favourites, such as the handsome but illiterate Cossack whom she made Field Marshal of the army. Government business was neglected, documents were left unread and decisions left unmade by the Empress. The Saxon ambassador wrote of her as 'not wanting to have her preferred use of time impeded, and not being able to abide government business, she kept away from it or considered it only with the utmost carelessness, often in annoyance that it inconvenienced her'. When she was moved to initiate legislation the purposes were personal and trivial – to prevent 'unpleasant sights such as funeral processions, or aged and infirm paupers' from offending the imperial eyes by their presence on the streets, for instance.

In 1741 the Cabinet set up by Anna was abolished, although later Elizabeth's inner circle of advisers were formally organised into a somewhat similar body, the Conference. This had considerable powers and was able to issue edicts in the name of the Empress. The Senate was restored to its previous status, but was seldom graced by Elizabeth's presence. In most years of her reign she did not trouble herself to attend even a single one of its meetings.

A further step in the total enserfment of the peasants was taken in 1744, when they were denied freedom to travel outside their villages without a passport from their lord. In 1760 a decree authorised the deportation of serfs to Siberia. This served a double purpose. Not only was it a means of punishing troublesome serfs, but it was an easy way of providing settlers for that inhospitable region.

6 Peter III 1761–2

Elizabeth died on Christmas Day, 1761 and was succeeded, unusually without dispute, by Peter, the son of her elder sister, Anna. The orphaned Grand Duke Peter (formerly Duke of Holstein and heir to the Swedish throne) had been brought over to Russia in his early teens, to be adopted by his aunt as her successor. After the customary conversion to Orthodoxy (he had been brought up as a Lutheran) he was formally recognised as heir to the Russian throne in November 1742. Three years later he was married to his cousin, the Princess Sophie of Anhalt-Zerbst, better known to history as Catherine the Great. By the time of his accession there was a son, Paul, of whom Peter may or may not have have been the father.

The *Memoirs* of Catherine are the source most frequently, and often uncritically, used for evaluating the reign of Peter III. Memoirs are notoriously unreliable primary sources. In this case they are positively misleading. During her lifetime Catherine reworked her *Memoirs* on at least six occasions. Each version was ever more flattering to her own appearance and achievements, and progressively less so to those of her husband and his aunt, the Empress Elizabeth. In one early version she describes Peter as handsome, obliging and well-mannered; in a later description of the same occasion he becomes 'a permanent patch on a beautiful face', hideous and repulsive to her. The tales which are told of Peter's drunkenness and buffoonery, his cruelties, his strange behaviour in private and in public stem mainly from Catherine, and are almost certainly greatly exaggerated. However, there seems to have been an element of truth in her allegations that he was mentally disturbed by 1762. The British ambassador, writing of Peter at the time of Catherine's *coup d'état*, described him as 'recently much altered':

1   Not only I, but several persons of sense and discernment thought they could perceive latterly in this Prince a considerable change from what he was for some months after his accession, and that the perpetual hurry in which he lived, and the flattery he received
5   from the vile people about him, had in some measure affected his understanding.

Peter was no hero himself, but he seems to have been a hero-worshipper. Most of his devotion was focused on Frederick II of Prussia, his uncle by marriage, and was expressed in an obsession with military activities such as drilling – first his toy soldiers and later the Guards. It was this admiration for Frederick and for all things Prussian which alienated him from Elizabeth at the time of the Seven Years War, and afterwards made him unpopular with many of his subjects.

Peter's reign was barely six months long, but during that time a number of liberalising measures were enacted. The penalties on the Old Believers and other religious dissidents were reduced; trade restrictions were relaxed and Peter the Great's hated Secret Chancellery (the Police Bureau) was abolished. This body investigated with great brutality all allegations of treason or sedition. In the preamble to the Manifesto abolishing it, Peter explained that the social and cultural conditions among the Russian people had so improved since the time of Peter the Great, that its work was no longer necessary. Its cases would therefore be transferred to a new department attached to the Senate.

*   The measure which has received the most attention from historians is the Manifesto on the Freedom of the Nobility, also issued in February 1762. The document had a long preamble, not dissimilar in character to that abolishing the Secret Chancellery. It began by rehearsing the difficulties faced by Peter the Great and the solutions he was compelled to adopt. Then, after describing how he had forced the nobles into military and civil service and ordered the education of their children, it continued:

1   It is true that in the beginning these demands were burdensome for the nobles . . . as they were forced to leave their homes and obliged against their will to serve in the army and other ways

and to send their children to school . . . These demands proved
5 advantageous . . . manners have improved, devotion and zeal for
military affairs have provided experienced generals; civil and
political concerns have produced many intelligent people . . .
We judge it, therefore, no longer necessary to compel the nobles
into service . . .
10 We grant freedom and liberty to the entire Russian nobility . . . from this moment and forever . . . No Russian noble
will ever be forced to serve against his will.

What did this 'grant of freedom and liberty' amount to? Serving
nobles of senior officer rank in the army or the bureaucracy could now
retire in times of peace with the consent of their superior officer or, in
some cases, of the Tsar himself. Nobles below senior officer rank were
required to have served at least twelve years before applying for
retirement. Retired nobles could travel abroad if they wished, but had
to return home if summoned. Failure to do so meant the confiscation
of their estates. Wealthy nobles would be allowed to educate their
children at home, but the state would continue compulsory education
of the children belonging to nobles with fewer than 1000 serfs (only
one per cent of the nobility had more than 1000 serfs). The final
clause applied moral pressure on the nobility to continue service on a
voluntary basis even when they were free to retire:

1 We hope that in return for this act, Russian nobles, realising
what great concern we have shown towards them and their
descendants, will continue to serve us loyally and zealously and
will not withdraw from our service; on the contrary that they
5 will seek the service eagerly and will continue in it as long as
possible . . . and will educate their children attentively in useful
knowledge. Those who will not perform service lead purposeless
lives . . . such people who are not concerned with the general
good, we recommend our faithful subjects to despise and avoid.
10 We will not allow such people access to our court, nor will we
tolerate their presence at public assemblies and festivals.

This Manifesto was, in the opinion of one modern historian, 'one
of the most important milestones in the modernisation of Russia'.
Others agree that 'it is difficult to exaggerate the importance of the
Edict of 1762 for Russia's social and cultural history', that the
Manifesto 'marks the nobles' emancipation from service' and that 'the
nobility achieved their cherished ambition of freedom from service'
which 'ceased to be compulsory'. However, some historians, both
British and Russian, do not share this view. They point out that the
decree did *not* abolish the obligation to serve — it merely reduced the
length of service by permitting retirement at the end of twelve years,

or after the attainment of a specified rank. The noted Russian historian V.O. Klyuchevsky asserted that the 'The law said; be so good, serve and teach your children, and nevertheless, he who does neither the one nor the other will be driven from society'. He belived that the phrases about 'freedom' for the nobility had been misunderstood, by both contemporary and later writers. Much of the difficulty centres on apparent contradictions within the Manifesto, and particularly the exact meaning of certain clauses, among them Clause 8:

1 Those nobles who are presently in our military service as soldiers and who have not attained the rank of senior officrer . . . should not be allowed to retire unless they have served twelve years in the army.

Did this apply only to those nobles *at present* (at this moment) serving, or did it apply to all nobles in a more general and less limited sense of *in the present age* (nowadays)? The Manifesto is known to have been drawn up on the direct orders of the Tsar in great haste, and its clarity of expression may simply have suffered in the drafting. On the other hand its phrasing may have been left deliberately vague to permit of such interpretation as seemed desirable from time to time. Certainly, the importance of the Manifesto must not be exaggerated. Its limited concessions need to be recognised as no more than another step towards ending the service conditions imposed by Peter the Great, a process begun by the Empress Anna in the 1730s and completed by Catherine the Great with her Charter of the Nobility in 1785. That said, the Manifesto *was* a significant step forward for the nobility in their pursuit of freedom from imperial control, even if its importance was not as great as some historians would make out.

  * In July 1762 Peter III was overthrown by a *coup d'état* staged by his wife Catherine and her supporters. Why did this happen so soon after his accession? Robert Keith, the British ambassador in St Petersburg, sent back to London a detailed account of events. In his considered opinion the causes of the 'revolution' were the secularisation of church lands; the remodelling of the army on Prussian lines and the severe discipline which the Tsar had introduced into the Guards Regiments which 'had been accustomed to great idleness and licence'; the decision by the Tsar to take his army into Germany on an expedition to recover from Denmark his family lands in Schleswig, 'a measure disagreeable to the whole nation'; and the 'sacrifice to his friend the King of Prussia of the conquests made by Russian arms' (in the Seven Years War). In addition,

1 Several other little circumstances, greatly exaggerated and artfully improved, contributed to the fall of this unhappy Prince

who had many excellent qualities, and who never did a violent or
cruel thing in the course of his short reign; but who by an
5 abhorrence to business, owing to a bad education, and the
unhappy choice of favourites . . . let everything run into confusion, and by a mistaken notion he had conceived of securing the
affections of the nation by the great favours he had so nobly
bestowed upon them after his first mounting the throne, fell into
10 an indolence and security that proved fatal to him.

Was this a correct assessment of the reasons for Peter's downfall? It
would seem so. Peter, who never made any secret of his preference for
Lutheranism, offended the Orthodox clergy on a number of occasions,

Catherine II's entry into St Petersburg

and seriously angered them by implementing a decree secularising
church lands made by the Empress Elizabeth shortly before her death.
He certainly threw away the Russian gains of the Seven Years War in
negotiations with his hero, Frederick II, obtaining in return only
promises of Prussian support for a proposed attack on Denmark to
recover Schleswig (part of Peter's family lands). It seemed to most
Russians that the Tsar was sacrificing their interests in favour of his
own family's ambitions – although it is possible to argue that success

in Schleswig would have given Russia greater influence in the Baltic. His attempts to reform and modernise the Guards and to restore discipline might have been accepted, if grudgingly. It appears to have been his insistence on a Prussian style of uniform and type of drill which caused the most resentment.

In her accession manifesto published immediately after the *coup*, Catherine justified her actions as necessary to counter 'the great dangers to which the Russian empire has actually been exposed' by the attacks on the Orthodox Church, the shameful peace made with the enemy, and the 'overturning of the domestic regulations which are the basis of the country's welfare'. The reasons given by Catherine more privately are rather different. In a letter written to Stanislas Poniatowski (her ex-lover and, later, King of Poland) two or three days after the *coup*, she declared that 'Peter III had lost what little intelligence he ever had. He shocked and offended everyone, wanted to change his religion, marry his mistress and arrest me.' But at the end of the letter she suddenly divulges what she thinks was the real reason for Peter's unpopularity: 'Everything was carried out on the principle of hatred of the foreigner; Peter III himself counted as such.' This might seem strange, coming from Catherine, herself a foreigner, but she appears, from her first arrival in the country, to have taken a conscious decision to become more Russian than the Russians. In this she was remarkably successful, unlike Peter who remained obstinately German in his sympathies and interests.

The details of the *coup* which deposed Peter are somewhat confused, but on 9 July 1762 Catherine was proclaimed Empress. Two days later Peter agreed to abdicate. He was then arrested and imprisoned in a country house near St Petersburg. What to do with him next was a problem. While he was still alive Catherine's position was extremely insecure. She had seized power by force with the backing of the Guards Regiments, as Anna and Elizabeth had done – but they had both had legitimate claims to the throne. Catherine had none. A week later, in mysterious circumstances, Peter was killed, allegedly in a drunken brawl, by one of his jailors. Catherine received the news of her husband's death with joy as 'evidence of God's divine intent'. The killing was covered up, and a manifesto was issued on 18 July to the effect that the Tsar had died of natural causes as the result of 'a haemorrhoidal colic'.

Contemporary English accounts describe Catherine's 'revolution' as 'a momentous constitutional change', pointing out that 'the most absolute power on earth is now held by an elective monarch'. But most Russian accessions since 1725 had been elective. There was nothing new in the means by which Catherine seized power – only in the lack of scruple she showed in deposing her husband (perhaps also disposing of him), and in her total disregard for the generally accepted

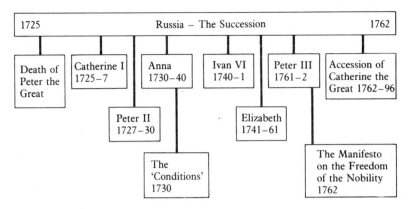

Summary – Russia 1725–63: Domestic Affairs

rights of inheritance. In June 1762 the elective process had simply reached its logical conclusion.

Making Notes on 'Russia 1725–63: Domestic Affairs'

It is unlikely that you will be faced with an examination question solely concerned with the period of Russian history 1725–63. However, information about constitutional and social developments during these years may be needed to answer a question on, for example, changes in the status and functions of the nobility between 1725 and 1785, or on changes in the nature of royal power in the same period. It is suggested, therefore, that instead of simply working straight through the chapter you use the following headings for your notes:

1. The Crown – why did it become more elective?
   what part did the nobility play in the process?
   what were their motives?
2. The Nobility – what concessions on service did they obtain for themselves?
   what additional rights did they obtain over their serfs?

Afterwards re-read the first paragraph of this chapter which gives the usually accepted historical view of the years 1725–63 in Russia. What conclusions have you reached about whether it is 'a fair and accurate representation'?

Source-based questions on 'Russia 1725–63: Domestic Affairs'

1 The Empress Anna and the Conditions

Read the extracts on pages 28 and 29, and the extract from the *Memoirs* of James Keith (page 28). Answer the following questions:

a) Explain what the writer meant by 'salutary laws' (page 28, line 4), 'make obeisance' (page 28, line 4) and 'the same prerogative as my ancestors' (page 29, line 2). (4 marks)

b) The authors of the four extracts differ in their opinions on absolute monarchy. Briefly categorise each of these four views as favourable/unfavourable to absolutism. What reason(s) are given for each of the views held? (8 marks)

c) The authors of the four extracts were from very different backgrounds – a magnate, a lesser noble, the Empress and a foreigner. (James Keith was one of many soldiers of fortune who took service in Russia and who, after Anna's succession, found himself promoted to Lieutenant-colonel in the Guards and in a position of some power at court.) How would you estimate the historical reliability of each of these extracts? (8 marks)

d) Give five reasons why, in the eighteenth century, the attempts to limit the powers of the Tsar were unsuccessful. (5 marks)

2 Peter III and the Manifesto to the Nobility

Read the extracts from the Manifesto on the Freedom of the Nobility on pages 34–6. Answer the following questions:

a) What reason does Peter III give for issuing the Manifesto (page 34, lines 4–9)? (2 marks)

b) What pressure does he apply to persuade the nobles to continue in service (page 35, lines 1–10)? Would such pressures be likely to be effective? Explain your answer. (5 marks)

c) What is the contradiction within the Manifesto in relation to the terms of service (page 35, lines 10–12 and page 36, lines 1–4)? (2 marks)

d) How significant was the Manifesto in the nobility's pursuit of freedom from service? (6 marks)

CHAPTER 4

Russia, Poland and the Ottoman Empire 1700–63: Foreign Affairs

Frequent confrontations and occasional alliances mark the relations between Russia, Poland and the Ottoman Empire as they jockeyed for position in eastern Europe during the first half of the eighteenth century. The national character and international standing of these states differed greatly. There was the rising power with an aggressive, expansionist foreign policy (Russia); the declining power at the start of a long retreat from Europe (the Ottoman Empire), and the once great power, now weak, defenceless and an easy prey for her neighbours (Poland). On the sidelines, sometimes helping, sometimes hindering, were Austria, Sweden and the up-and-coming state of Prussia.

* The last two decades of the seventeenth century had brought a series of severe military disasters to the Ottomans. These culminated in the humiliating Treaty of Karlowitz in 1699, by which they had lost portions of their Balkan possessions to Austria, Venice and Poland. A year later another treaty had made peace between the Ottomans and Russia, and had left the important Ottoman port of Azov on the Black Sea in Russian hands. The loss of Azov had been a serious blow to the Ottomans. For the first time it had given Russia direct access to the Black Sea (see map on page 45). It was to be a source of anxiety to the Ottomans for the remainder of the eighteenth century that, as their influence in the Crimea began to wane, Russian influence both there and in the Caucasus was increasing.

The new Sultan Ahmed III (1703–30) wisely recognised that his country was in no state to embark on an aggressive foreign policy. Therefore, he contented himself with strengthening his standing army, expanding the navy and improving the coastal defences. He was the pleasure-loving, extravagant Sultan whose reign is known as the Tulip Period. It was a time of intellectual and cultural development which, for the first time in Ottoman history, borrowed heavily from European artistic and literary traditions. Along the Golden Horn new and splendid palaces with western furnishings and with fountains and ornamental gardens modelled on Fontainbleau were the scene of elaborate court festivities. Music, dancing and poetry provided the entertainment, but the chief interest of the Sultan and the Ruling Class was the growing of tulips. Fortunes were spent on rare bulbs, possession of which could be the passport to high office and the Sultan's favour. Ahmed was not at all warlike, preferring a life of indolence and luxury. He resisted pressure from the Ottoman Empire's old ally, France, to intervene on the side of Sweden at the beginning of the Great Northern War. His insistence on continued Ottoman neutrality was an important factor in saving Russia from disaster in 1707–8 at the time of the Swedish invasion, when the Ottomans' vassal, the Khan of the Crimea, and his Tartar army were prevented from joining the Swedes. If they had been allowed to do so the outcome of the battle of Poltava might have been very different.

1 The Great Northern War 1700–21

The Great Northern War was a Russian bid for power in the Baltic. On his journey through Poland in 1698 Peter the Great had met and plotted with Augustus II to make war on Sweden. In his capacity as Elector of Saxony, Augustus allied himself with Russia and Denmark to fight a war in which Poland, although not directly involved, was to become the prime victim. In 1700 Augustus attacked Swedish Livonia, mainly for reasons of personal aggrandisement, although it could be argued that a Saxon military presence in Riga would have made it easier to enforce the King's authority in lawless Lithuania. The attack failed, and at about the same time the Russians were defeated by a much smaller Swedish army. Peter the Great regrouped his army during the winter, before moving back into the Baltic area, where this time he was much more successful. By 1703 the whole area of the River Neva was in Russian hands and at its mouth the foundations of the new city of St Petersburg were being laid.

Meanwhile, in 1701, Charles XII of Sweden had successfully occupied the Polish Duchy of Courland. From there, in 1702, he took the easy option rather than invade Russia. He marched his armies, largely unopposed, straight through Poland from north to south, occupying Wilno, Warsaw and Cracow on the way and defeating the Polish cavalry in one of the few set battles of the campaign. This invasion was to prove only the start of Augustus's troubles. Rival armed Confederations were formed by the Polish *szlachta*, adding civil war to foreign occupation. One Confederation was pro-Saxon and relied heavily on Russian money and men for support; the other, which had Swedish backing, suddenly produced its own contender for the Polish throne in 1704 – Stanislas Leszczynski, a cultured, jovial Polish nobleman from Wielkopolska. For three years Augustus was harried round the Republic, advancing and retreating ineffectually before the Swedish army, until in 1706 Charles XII marched into Saxony itself. There Augustus was forced to make a formal renunciation of the Polish throne in favour of Leszczynski, who had already been proclaimed king. After nearly seven years of campaigning the war proper was no nearer an end. Charles XII therefore decided that his only hope of victory over Peter the Great was to take the dangerous gamble of invading Russia. Leaving Leszczynski in charge of Poland, he set out from Grodno with 50,000 men in January 1708.

When Charles arrived in Russia he found the country well prepared and ready to resist. After a long, hot and largely inactive summer, he abandoned his plan to advance on Moscow, and instead turned south where he hoped to find help from the Hetman (military commander) of the Ukraine, Ivan Mazeppa. He also hoped – over-optimistically as it turned out – that the Sultan would provide him with aid. Mazeppa did agree to join him, but the extent of Cossack support was less than expected. In the spring of 1709 the Swedes besieged the fortress of Poltava to the east of Kiev, and there in July they were heavily defeated by a Russian army twice the size of their own.

Poltava was not only a turning point in the war. It also tipped the balance of power in eastern Europe in favour of Russia for the first time. Russian troops quickly occupied Estonia and Livonia, consolidating their foothold on the Baltic shore, and then drove Leszczynski out of Poland. Swedish influence in Poland was at an end – Russian influence was about to begin. In 1710 the Russians restored Augustus to his throne as their client-king in return for a formal Polish acknowledgement of Russian rights to Kiev and Poland's 'eastern lands', theoretically ceded in 1686 but not fully accepted by Poland in fact. The increasing dependence of Poland on her Russian neighbour during the next half-century is one of the dominant themes of the period. After 1710, Poland can hardly be said to have had a 'foreign policy – at least not one of her own – for all was done at the behest of her 'protectors'. The Republic became at most a passive spectator, more often a victim of international events increasingly beyond her control.

* In Istanbul there were grave misgivings about the implications of the Russian victory at Poltava, and about the advisability of continuing the current policy of Ottoman neutrality. An unwelcome complication for the Sultan was the unexpected arrival on Ottoman soil of Charles XII and Mazeppa, who had escaped after the battle and had fled across Poland. Russian troops stationed there had pursued the fugitives south, and in doing so had crossed the Ottoman frontier. The diplomatic situation was suddenly very delicate, and it was with some reluctance that the Sultan granted asylum to Charles and his ally. The Tsar demanded Charles's expulsion – the Sultan refused. Peter offered a few minor amendments to the treaty of 1700, and in return the Sultan agreed to send Charles back to Sweden, if he were given a safe conduct by the Tsar and accompanied by an Ottoman military escort. Charles refused to go. The Tsar sent an ultimatum insisting on immediate departure. On the day the ultimatum reached Istanbul in December 1710, the Sultan declared war on Russia. In doing this, he was not so much concerned to protect Charles, who was proving a troublesome and unwelcome guest, as to signify Ottoman

opposition to Russian interference in the Empire's affairs. So began the long conflict between the two powers which was to continue intermittently for the next 200 years.

2 Russo-Ottoman War: The Pruth Campaign 1711

Peter the Great, who had already announced his intention of 'freeing' the Balkan Orthodox Christians from 'the yoke of the infidels', obtained promises of military support from the Ottoman vassal princes of Moldavia and Wallachia, together with the provision of food and forage for any invading Russian army of 'liberation'. He also anticipated that there would be support from a general uprising of Orthodox peasants against their Moslem rulers.

In May 1711 the Ottoman army, with the Grand Vezir at its head, marched out of Istanbul towards the Balkans at the same time as Peter, his wife and an army of 40,000 infantry and 14,000 cavalry were advancing through Poland and across the River Pruth into Moldavia. The promised popular support there for the invaders did not materialise and food for men and horses ran short. When Peter learned that the Grand Vezir was not, as he believed, 60 miles away but was already close at hand with an army 130,000 strong, he attempted to recross the river, but was caught and surrounded before he could do so. The Ottomans had him at their mercy. At the very least they could have demanded unconditional surrender, followed by major territorial concessions. But the Grand Vezir hesitated. He had severe supply problems of his own, was uncertain about the loyalty of the Tartar troops and believed, wrongly, that Russian reinforcements were near by. He therefore settled for a quick negotiated peace, before he could be forced to retreat through lack of supplies.

The Treaty of the Pruth agreed among other things that Russia would return all lands conquered from the Ottomans, including Azov, would refrain from interfering in Polish affairs, and would provide Charles XII with a safe passage back to Sweden. The treaty, despite its limitations, was well received in Istanbul, where it was felt to wipe out the memory of recent past failures. However, trouble soon arose because the Russians were slow in putting the terms of the treaty into effect. There was a delay in recalling Russian troops from Poland, where their continued presence led the Sultan, with French encouragement, to threaten fresh hostilities. There were further difficulties about sending Charles home and in April 1713 the Sultan again declared war on Russia. Nothing came of it, and two months later a new 25-year peace treaty, confirming the arrangements made at the Pruth, was concluded between the two countries. Peter the Great finally gave a safe conduct to Charles XII, who left the Ottoman Empire in 1714 and returned to Sweden.

The Russo-Ottoman peace treaty did not bring the Great Northern

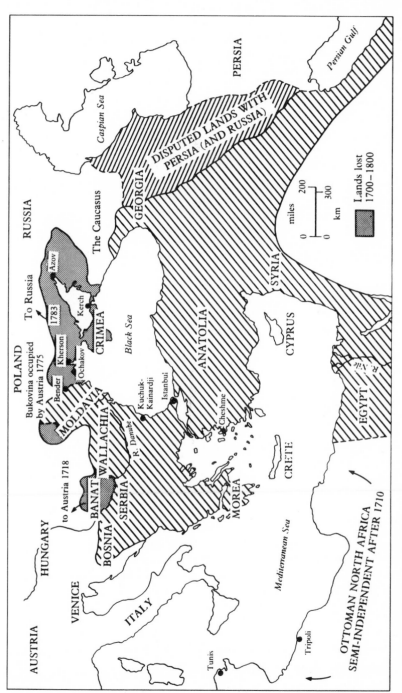

The Ottoman Empire in the eighteenth century

War to an end. Hostilities continued in the Baltic until, in 1718, Charles was killed while attacking a Danish fortress. In 1721 a peace treaty was finally concluded at Nystadt. This confirmed to Russia her gains on the Baltic, but left Russia and Sweden on good enough terms to conclude a treaty of mutual defence three years later. With the eclipse of Sweden, Russia had become the dominant power in the Baltic.

3 The Ottoman War with Venice and Austria 1714–17

While Russia and Sweden were continuing their war in the Baltic, the Ottomans had plunged into war with Venice at the end of 1714, with the aim of recovering territory lost in 1699. The Morea was quickly recaptured in 1715, and the Grand Vezir, over-confident after this easy victory, persuaded the Sultan the following year to declare war on Austria, the Venetians' ally. After a severe defeat in August 1716, when the Grand Vezir himself was killed, a series of Austrian victories, which culminated in the capture of Belgrade, led the Ottomans to make peace with Austria.

In 1717 the Treaty of Passarowitz was signed with the Austrians on the basis of *uti possedetis* (each side to keep what it actually held at the date of the treaty). The Ottomans had not only failed to recover their 1699 losses, but were forced to agree a new frontier with Austria and to cede to her Belgrade, the Banat and part of Serbia. The Ottomans were more successful in their treaty with Venice, and retained the Morea. It had been an expensive war for the Sultan, and had revealed serious deficiencies in the leadership and organisation of the Ottoman army, which, being short of modern firearms, still relied heavily on the mass charge and hand-to-hand fighting. The Ottomans had been consistently defeated by the smaller, more mobile, better equipped and better led Austrian army. How to reform and modernise their army was a problem which confronted successive sultans for the remainder of the century – a problem which they never completely solved.

4 Persian Affairs

Concerned with securing his southern frontier against possible Ottoman attack, Peter sent an emissary to investigate the internal situation in Persia in 1715. Five years later a rebel Afghan invasion of Persia led the Shah to send an appeal for help to the Ottoman Sultan as the most important of the Moslem rulers. The appeal was ignored and no help was sent, perhaps because of past religious conflicts between the Sunn'ite (orthodox) Ottomans and the Shi'ite (heretical) Persians. The Shah's flight two years later resulted in a series of popular uprisings in and around the Caucasus and the Caspian Sea, and in 1722, with the end of the Great Northern War, Peter felt able to take advantage of the chaos in the region. He moved his troops to Astrakhan during the summer and launched a campaign along the western shore of the Caspian Sea. He captured the important harbour of Darband and highhandedly ordered the Ottomans not to approach the area. In return for an offer of military assistance against the Afghans, a new shah formally ceded to Russia all the Persian provinces bordering the Caspian Sea to the south and west. But these areas had at one time been part of the Ottoman Empire. The Ottomans could not allow them to fall unchallenged into infidel hands. The Sultan and his Grand Vezir were stirred into action.

In 1723, as Peter continued his campaign, the Ottomans declared war on Persia, invaded Georgia and then occupied a number of Persian provinces. As a result, war again threatened between Russia and the Ottoman Empire, but the French ambassador was able to mediate a peace settlement. A frontier between the two powers was agreed which provided for a dismemberment of the disputed Persian provinces. The Russians remained in occupation of the Caucasus and the southern shores of the Caspian Sea, while the Ottomans kept Georgia, Azerbaijan and the other contested areas. This was the only occasion on which Russia and the Ottoman Empire agreed to partition the territory of a neighbouring state, and a Moslem one at that. However, neither side benefited for long from their intervention – in 1730 the Ottomans were forced by a new and energetic shah to surrender a large part of their territorial gains, and by 1735 the Russians had also agreed to give up their Persian possessions.

Despite the short duration of this particular Russian involvement in Persia, the Ottomans continued to worry about Russian ambitions there, as well as about the threat of Russian domination in the area of the Caspian Sea and the probability of a Russian presence in and around the Black Sea. They were also increasingly concerned about Russian intervention in Poland. Russian activity in any of these areas constituted a potential threat to the security of the Ottoman Empire. The Sultan and his government would have agreed wholeheartedly with the comments of a Russian diplomat that:

1 the greater part of our neighbours view very unfavourably the good position in which it has pleased God to place Russia; they would be delighted should an occasion present itself to imprison us once more in our earlier obscurity and if they seek our alli-
5 ance it is rather through fear and hate than through feelings of friendship.

However, any return of Russia to a position of international obscurity could be no more than a piece of wishful thinking after 1721. Russia was now emerging as a major European power, despite the fact that the others might be unwilling to admit it. As one Russian official told Peter the Great at the celebrations held to mark the signing of the Treaty of Nystadt:

1 By your tireless labours and under your guidance we have been led from the shades of ignorance to the stage of glory before the world. We have been led from nothing to life, and we have rejoined the company of political nations.

There could be no going back.

5 The War of the Polish Succession 1733–8

Peter the Great had made a lengthy visit to Poland during Augustus II's enforced absence at the time of the Great Northern War. He had not been impressed with what he found there – the term 'Polish Anarchy' first appears in Russian documents of this time. After his restoration in 1710 Augustus quickly came into open conflict with the *szlachta* over possible constitutional reforms, and was driven out of Poland by an armed Confederation. Peter the Great was unwilling to see his client-king defeated and offered to mediate between Augustus and his subjects. The mediation, backed by 18,000 Russian troops, was successful and an agreement was drawn up. The *Sejm* was persuaded to accept an upper limit of 24,000 men for the Polish army. The mediators pointed out that this was quite sufficient to defend Poland as Russian troops would remain in the country as 'friendly protectors'. Peter undertook to guarantee the peace settlement between king and *szlachta*, but in a form which would give him the right to interfere in Polish affairs as and when he wished, and would prevent any alteration to the Polish constitution without Russian consent. The Dumb (or Silent) *Sejm* at its meeting in January 1717, surrounded by Russian soldiers, meekly accepted these proposals and surrendered Poland's independence by the Treaty of Warsaw. Poland had become a Russian protectorate. As the French representative in Danzig remarked shortly afterwards, 'the Muscovites claim to be in command wherever they happen to be, pretending that everything they can find belongs to them and that they can behave as they like'.

When Augustus II died in 1733 he was eventually succeeded by his son, another Augustus, but only after a disputed election in which Stanislas Leszczynski, this time backed by France, was successful. However, Leszczynski was quickly dispossessed by Russian troops sent in by the Empress Anna 'in case of the Republic not taking with good grace her decision that Augustus should be elected'. The armed Confederations – usual after a disputed royal election – were quickly formed as a prelude to civil war, the fighting on this occasion being augmented by peasant uprisings. However, there was little serious military action in Poland, apart from the landing at Danzig (Gdansk) of a small French contingent, in support of Leszczynski who had taken refuge there. Before the city fell to the Russians in May 1734, Leszczynski managed to escape disguised as a peasant, but his bid for the Polish throne was over even before this. The Russians had arranged for Augustus III to be crowned in Cracow four months earlier. Although anti-Russian activity continued in Poland into 1736, it was very sporadic and presented no serious problems to the occupying Russian army.

The War of the Polish Succession proper took place outside Poland. It was fought in western Europe by non-Polish troops and over non-Polish issues. The Poles' future was being determined for them by others. They and their king were mere pawns in an international power game. The fact that by its outcome the war eventually settled who should be king of Poland was merely incidental to most of the players.

The real issues of the war concerned French prestige in Europe. The Polish election crisis was manipulated by the French government to provide an excuse to attack Austria in order to acquire the strategically important Duchy of Lorraine. Once the fighting in Poland was nearly over Russian troops could be spared from there, and 13,000 of them marched across Europe to the Rhine to the assistance of Austria, the first time that Russian troops had been sent into western Europe on active service. Almost immediately, however, Austria decided to sue for peace, and by the end of 1735 had signed a preliminary agreement with France. As part of a general exchange, Austria surrendered Lorraine in return for French acceptance of the Pragmatic Sanction (see page 61). Leszczynski got his consolation prize, a life-interest in Lorraine, and set up as a model of the Enlightenment there, presiding over a court where he entertained gourmets and *philosophes* from all over Europe until his death in 1766.

In a minor clause of the final peace treaty, Augustus III's *de facto* position as King of Poland since 1734 was formally accepted by the major powers, who thus tacitly acknowledged Russian supremacy over Polish affairs.

6 The Russo-Ottoman War 1736–9

With Poland quiescent by 1736 and the War of the Polish Succession over to all intents and purposes, Russia was free to concentrate on her southern frontier. For Russia any advance in that area would serve two purposes. By occupying the Crimea, the Tartars, who were Ottoman vassals, could be brought under control and an end made to their troublesome raids into Russian territory, while at the same time Russia would come a step nearer the long-desired transformation of the Black Sea from an Ottoman lake into a Russian one.

Russo-Austrian cooperation during the War of the Polish Succession had led to the signing of a secret agreement between the two countries. According to its terms, Austria agreed to join Russia in any future war against the Ottomans in return for an equal share of the spoils. In 1736 the Ottomans themselves were not averse to the idea of a further war with Russia. They had been tempted to declare war in 1734 in support of the French candidate, Leszczynski, as King of Poland, and only commitments in Persia had prevented them from doing so. France was an Ottoman ally of long-standing and was the Empire's major contact with western Europe. The connection between the two countries dated back to the early sixteenth century when it had been based on a shared hatred of the Habsburgs. Although the alliance was no longer so strong, it remained an important element in Ottoman foreign policy. The French ambassador still retained considerable influence in Istanbul, and it was to France that the Ottomans turned whenever mediation or support was required. Despite the Ottomans' usual unreadiness, France urged war when, early in 1736, reports reached the Sultan of a new agreement between Russia and Austria to divide up part of the Ottoman Empire, allocating the Crimea and Azov to Russia and Bosnia and Herzegovina to Austria. An ultimatum from Russia followed, containing trumped up accusations of Ottoman violations of the Pruth treaty. It was rejected by the Sultan. War became inevitable and was formally declared in May 1736.

* Ever since the military disasters which had overtaken the Ottomans at the end of the seventeenth century, the Ruling Class had tried to find ways of halting or even reversing the decline in Ottoman power and prestige. A minority of them realised that if the Empire was to recover its former greatness, it must make use of some European ideas and techniques. They saw that the traditional response – simply to make existing practices work more efficiently regardless of changing circumstances – was no longer a practicable solution. They never advocated anything very extreme, but *any* changes at all were opposed by the conservative members of the Ruling Class, particularly those in the *ulema* (the religious hierarchy). The latter's opposition was based on a saying of the Prophet Mohammed that 'The worst things are those that are novelties, every novelty is an innovation, every innovation is an error, and every error leads to Hell-fire'. Given the importance of the *sheriat* (Islamic religious law) in Ottoman life, change of any kind was very difficult to achieve. As a result all attempts at reform before 1763, and most of those afterwards, were basically traditional, largely superficial and usually transitory. The Sultans and grand vezirs were able to achieve little beyond a certain modernisation of military training and weaponry. Mahmud I was sufficiently enterprising to bring in the first of many European experts, the Comte de Bonneval, who had plans for reforming the

whole Ottoman army along French and Austrian lines. This was much too radical an idea for the Janissaries and was abandoned. Instead he was appointed in 1732 to revive the old Bombardier corps, which had fallen into disuse. It was reformed along European lines and for a while, masquerading under an old name, it excited no opposition; but as it came into active service, the Janissaries became aware of their own technological shortcomings. They managed to have Bonneval exiled and his Bombardier corps and School of Military Engineering closed down. The traditionalists had triumphed.

* Therefore, despite their enthusiasm for war with Russia, it is perhaps not surprising that the Ottomans had not even mobilised the army when war was declared. In any case they expected the initial Russian attack to be in the Balkans and immediately sent large numbers of Tartars to hold the area of the Danube until the main army could arrive. However, the Russians had been fully mobilised before the war began, and they decided to make a surprise attack on the Crimea rather than the Balkans. The Russian army quickly advanced and recaptured Azov. But their very success was their undoing. Their supply lines became over-extended, and there was no hope of living off the land which they had destroyed as they went along. They fell victim to famine and disease and had to evacuate the whole peninsula at the end of the summer.

Russia's ally, Austria, was initially very successful in the Balkans, but soon lost all her early conquests. She became disheartened with the war and made a separate peace with the Ottomans by which she surrendered even the gains she had made in 1717 (see page 45). The Russians also made a number of important gains in the Balkans, and at one time it even seemed probable that Moldavia would be incorporated into the Russian Empire. But supply and other problems eventually forced the Russians to accept French offers of mediation. By the Treaty of Belgrade which ended the war in 1739, the Russians relinquished all their Balkan gains and gave up, for the time being, their ambitions in the Black Sea region, although they were allowed to keep Azov. The Russians had lost 100,000 men and had expended vast sums of money for very little result.

In 1740 The Ottoman Empire embarked on a long period of peace in Europe, and was not involved in any conflicts there until renewed hostilities with Russia broke out in the reign of Catherine the Great (see page 132). In many ways this long peace was a disaster for the Ottomans. Without the challenge of war, reforms were abandoned and the Empire sank back into lethargy.

7 Diplomatic Developments

In December 1740 Frederick II of Prussia launched an unprovoked attack on Austrian Silesia and catapulted Europe into the War of the Austrian Succession. By occupying Silesia before Augustus III could think of doing so, Frederick weakened both Saxony and Poland by driving a wedge between them, and gained both strategically and economically from the acquisition.

Russia remained on the sidelines during the war. She was unwilling to be committed to military intervention on behalf of Austria, her ally of the 1730s, because of domestic problems following on the death of the Empress Anna in 1740. Elizabeth, once established as Empress in 1741, turned on the Swedes who had supported her in her bid for the throne, and forced them to cede part of Finland to Russia. This would provide increased protection for St Petersburg against any Swedish attack in the future.

The years after 1748 were a time of change in the diplomatic and political alignment of the Great Powers. Russian ministers were unreasonably offended at being excluded from the 1748 peace negotiations at Aix-la-Chapelle at the end of a war (the War of the Austrian Succession) in which they had played no active part. As a result, relations with France deteriorated, because the Russians blamed the French for the exclusion. Nevertheless, a strong pro-French party flourished alongside a pro-Austrian one at Elizabeth's court. Their common ground with each other and with the Empress was a hatred of Prussia. Frederick II's temporary occupation of Saxony in 1746 had caused great resentment and some anxiety in Russia. While Prussia had not yet directly challenged Russian authority in Poland, her growing importance in northern Germany was a threat to Russian influence in the eastern Baltic. To counter this threat Russia had made a new defensive anti-Prussian alliance with Austria in 1746.

This anti-Prussian feeling led the Russian Chancellor to propose a partition of Prussia, to be carried out with help from Austria, Saxony and Poland, which would leave only a small rump state of Prussia – although even that would be a Russian satellite. Austria would be rewarded with the return of Silesia, while Poland would have East Prussia and in return would cede Courland and all the lands east of the Dvina and Dneiper rivers to Russia. Nothing came of this particular idea, but the Russians were not alone in planning the destruction of Prussia. The Austrian Chancellor, Kaunitz, was working for a European coalition against Prussia. He began by encouraging renewed Austrian friendship with her 'natural ally' Russia, and continued by arranging in 1756 an alliance with Austria's long standing enemy, France. This was a startling development, so unexpected that it came to known as the 'Diplomatic Revolution' (see page 65).

In March 1756 Russia began planning a war against Prussia, to be carried out with Austrian and perhaps also French help. A Russian army of 330,000 began to mobilise – though it was a notoriously slow and laborious process. The Austrians, whose troops numbered nearly

180,000, also began mobilisation. At the end of August, Frederick II, faced with Russian and Austrian troops gathered along his borders, made a pre-emptive strike and invaded Saxony. The Saxon forces were quickly surrounded, and as quickly surrendered, while Augustus III retired to the safety of Poland. These events activated the Austro-French alliance and committed France to war with Prussia. Frederick had, by his own actions, completed the European coalition against him. The Seven Years War had begun.

8 The Seven Years War 1756–63

In February 1757 Russia and Austria concluded an offensive alliance against Prussia. In May a similar alliance was signed by Austria and France. There was, however, no similar treaty between France and Russia. Russia and France were bound to each other only through their alliances with Austria, and their original enmity, never entirely overcome, surfaced from time to time during the next six years to the disadvantage of the allied war effort. The war aims of the allies were diverse – Austria hoped to recover Silesia, while Russia aspired to acquire new land and influence in the Baltic region. France was more concerned with victory in her colonial conflict with Britain, and played little direct part in the European struggle after it became clear in 1758 that Prussia was not going to be quickly or easily defeated. The Empress Elizabeth, now in a rapidly declining state of health, became obsessed by her hatred of Prussia and by a desire to acquire East Prussia, which she planned either to annexe or to exchange for part of Poland. By 1761 both France and Austria wished to end the war, but Elizabeth insisted that it should continue until Prussia was destroyed.

Frederick, whose position finally became desperate despite his brilliant generalship, was saved from total disaster by the death of Elizabeth early in 1762. Her successor, Peter III, was a Prussophile. He immediately signed a peace treaty with his hero Frederick, and followed it with a Russo-Prussian alliance. On her accession six months later Catherine II refused to ratify the alliance with Prussia, but agreed to remain neutral in the war, which finally came to an end in 1763.

9 Poland

A minor problem which Catherine inherited from her predecessors concerned the Polish fief of Courland. Count Biron, who had been the favourite of the Empress Anna and to whom the Duchy of Courland had been granted by Augustus III in 1733, had eventually become regent for the infant Ivan VI. After the *coup* which brought Elizabeth to the throne, he had been exiled to Siberia in 1741. In 1758 Elizabeth had given her support to an attempt by Augustus as overlord of Courland to transfer the fief to his own son, Charles. One of the first acts of Peter III in 1762 had been to withdraw support from Charles as a Saxon, and therefore anti-Prussian holder of the Duchy. Biron had been recalled from exile. However, he had not been restored to Courland but had been forced to give up his claim, being replaced by a member of Peter's own German family. Within a few days of her accession Catherine had ordered her envoy in Courland to support the restoration of Biron, who had agreed 'to be attentive to Russian requests'. By the spring of 1763 Russian troops had driven Charles out of Courland, which, although it was still nominally a Polish fief, had become to all intents and purposes a Russian protectorate on the shores of the Baltic.

In late 1763 the visit of an Ottoman envoy to Prussia alarmed Catherine. There was talk of a Prusso-Ottoman alliance. Catherine was persuaded of the need for a speedy *rapprochement* with Frederick, particularly as Augustus III and his heir both died before the end of the year. This left the delicate problem of a new king for Poland. To solve it, the Russian quarrel with Prussia was patched up in 1764 by a defensive alliance (see page 69). The way was being paved for their joint territorial expansion, along with Austria, in the partitions of Poland.

10 Overview

The first half of the eighteenth century was a time of varied fortunes for the three powers. For Russia it was a time of expansion. There were territorial gains from Sweden in the north along the Baltic shore by Peter the Great and Elizabeth, and the foundation of the new city of St Petersburg, Russia's 'window on the west'. In the south, conquests from the Ottoman Empire took Russia a step nearer to the Black Sea. Russia's western frontier had been secured by turning Poland into a client state to form a useful buffer zone against the rest of Europe. By the middle of the century Russia was firmly established as a Great Power.

As Russian power and international prestige increased, those of Poland and the Ottoman Empire declined. Under Augustus II and Augustus III Poland's capacity for independent action in foreign affairs was progressively reduced as she fell further and further under Russian domination. For most of the period her role was a passive one. She played little or no part in the War of the Polish Succession, but was simply the victim to be fought over by others. The Ottoman Empire, after disastrous wars against Austria and Russia in the earlier part of the century, recovered slightly with the Treaty of Belgrade in 1739, and ended the period with 20 years of peace. This was to prove a mixed blessing. When war with Russia began again in 1768, the Ottomans were in no way ready for it.

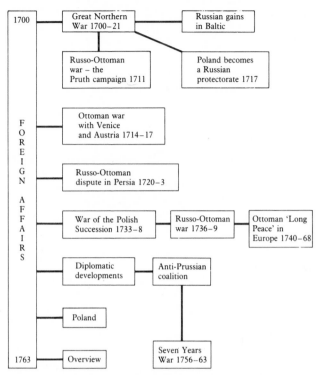

Summary – Russia, Poland and the Ottoman Empire 1700–63: Foreign Affairs

Making Notes on *'Russia, Poland and the Ottoman Empire 1700–63: Foreign Affairs'*

This chapter traces the relations between the three countries from the beginning of the century to 1763. While making your notes you will probably find it useful to build up a time-chart recording the names and dates of the main events. Arrange the information in three columns, one for each of the three powers. Allow enough space for it to cover the whole of the eighteenth century. You will then be able to add further information as you work through the remainder of the book, providing you with a brief comparative summary of events.

You may find it helpful to follow the pattern of headings within the chapter when making your notes.

CHAPTER 5

Diplomacy in the Eighteenth Century

Changes in the organisation and conduct of diplomatic affairs throughout Europe had a profound effect on international relations during the eighteenth century.

1 Diplomatic Organisation

By the early eighteenth century the foundations of modern diplomacy had been established in Europe. Special embassies and envoys-extraordinary had always been sent out from one country to another to announce momentous tidings (the death of a sovereign for instance) or to carry out negotiations for war or peace. Such missions, by their very nature, were occasional and temporary. From the fifteenth century onwards, however, Venice and other Italian city states began to maintain representatives in other western European states on a more or less permanent basis. By the early sixteenth century Venetian *bailos* were to be found as far afield as Istanbul, although there their function was as much commercial as diplomatic. In the course of the sixteenth century European diplomatic contacts continued to grow in number and scope. Envoys usually conducted a regular and often extensive correspondence with their own governments, and their despatches and reports, carefully preserved in the official archives, provide an important source of information for historians.

Diplomatic appointments were not, however, necessarily reciprocal at first. It was Louis XIV of France who began the practice of a regular exchange of permanent resident diplomats with foreign courts. Other European sovereigns quickly followed his example. The practice spread to eastern Europe. In 1702 there were only four foreign diplomats resident in Russia. In 1719 there were eleven. In 1699 there had been no permanent Russian representative attached to any European court. By 1721 there were 21. However, the Ottoman Empire remained aloof from the general trend; not until 1793 did the Sultan establish permanent embassies abroad, although English, Dutch, French, Austrian and Russian as well as Venetian representatives had long been accredited to the Porte (the Ottoman government). There were other countries, too, whose diplomatic representation abroad was very limited. One of these was Poland under Saxon rule in the first half of the eighteenth century. Augustus II sent out on behalf of Poland only 38 diplomatic missions, all of them temporary, in the 36 years of his reign, and few foreign representatives ever visited Warsaw, going instead to the Saxon capital of Dresden.

Foreign policy became increasingly dependent on a network of permanent embassies, which served to bring states into much closer day-to-day contact than ever before. These embassies carried out diplomatic negotiations and a wide range of other activities. The basis of the modern state system was being established. As French methods had set the new pattern, French gradually came to replace Latin as the language of international communication. All major treaties after Utrecht (1713) were in French. Most diplomats used French to communicate with their governments – although Catherine the Great issued special orders that despatches from her representatives abroad were to be written in Russian.

a) Immunity

Even before the end of the seventeenth century, it was usual for a diplomat and his household to be accorded special protection and immunity by the government of the country to which he was accredited. It was a way of ensuring good permanent relations between states, providing a ready channel of communication and reducing the likelihood of misunderstanding or friction. There were exceptions to this generally accepted rule. In the Ottoman Empire a foreign ambassador was likely to be seized and imprisoned in the Castle of the Seven Towers in Istanbul as a token that war had been declared by the Porte against that of the ambassador. This happened in 1768 to the Russian ambassador at the outbreak of the Russo-Turkish war. Some years earlier, in 1733, the French ambassador in Warsaw was imprisoned in the castle at Danzig for three years. However, he might be said to have forfeited his diplomatic immunity, for he had been involved in a number of dubious practices in support of the French candidate in the Polish royal election. Foreign ambassadors in Russia, too, often found themselves in difficulties, while Russian ambassadors themselves, even in the latter part of the eighteenth century, frequently preferred the use of force to that of diplomacy. The activities of Repnin and his successors in Poland during the partitions are a prime example of this (see page 74).

b) Political Espionage

It was important that information should be speedily, and secretly, exchanged between an ambassador and his government, but this was not always easy to arrange. The safest way was to send documents by special couriers, who also enjoyed diplomatic immunity, but who were expensive. It was cheaper, but much slower and certainly more dangerous, to use the ordinary postal services. Mail being sent home by the French ambassador in Warsaw was personally seized and read by his Prussian counterpart in 1758. This was an exceptional and shocking case, which highlighted the need to use coded messages, a precaution which most embassies had already begun to take. More than 20 years earlier, Sir Edward Finch, sent as British ambassador to Poland in 1725–6 to help the Protestants of Thorn (see page 69), was using a simple random number substitution cypher to report to London on how he was beset with difficulties, not the least of which was the placing of a guard at his door by the Polish authorities. Many states (Britain, France and Austria in particular) maintained highly successful *cabinets noirs* – official government departments created for the specific purpose of intercepting and copying despatches sent and received by foreign diplomats.

In addition to this official information-gathering service, there were numerous opportunities for less reputable activities. Diplomats and their servants were often corrupt, and money could sometimes buy state secrets from them. Thugut, the Austrian representative in Istanbul from 1769 to 1775 was an agent in French pay. During these six years he regularly sent confidential information to his French counterpart in the city. (Although his activities became public knowledge, they did not prevent his later promotion to Austrian Foreign Minister, and aroused no adverse comment among his contemporaries – in fact, rather the contrary.) Although the importance of political espionage must not be exaggerated, it was a significant element in the conduct of international relations. France and Austria seem to have been particularly active in this field. At precisely the same time as Thugut was working as a French agent in Istanbul, the entire correspondence of the British ambassador there was being copied by a servant and sent to the French ambassador, while, simultaneously, the French ambassador in Vienna was being supplied by another informer with confidential information about Austrian intentions. The British minister in Vienna had to complain that he only received the *cabinet noir* copies of his government's despatches, while the originals were sent to the Austrian Chancellor Kaunitz! The most serious case of political espionage in the eighteenth century, if judged by its repercussions, was the betrayal of Saxon government documents to the Prussians by a venal clerk in 1756. This disclosure of state secrets was a contributory factor in Frederick II's decision to invade Saxony in 1756.

c) Secret Diplomacy

Secret diplomacy at the highest level became a feature of foreign affairs from the mid-eighteenth century. The precedent was set by France, where Louis XV directed his *secret du roi* (the king's secret) which bypassed ministers and official channels. In an attempt to get his cousin, the Prince de Conti, chosen as candidate for the Polish throne, Louis instructed French agents to work secretly to this end. In 1752 the French ambassador in Warsaw, acting on the King's orders, became the centre of a web of secret intrigues to rebuild the seventeenth-century 'barrier' of Sweden, Poland and the Ottoman Empire to check Russian expansion and to restrain Austria.

d) Training

Only major states were entitled to exchange (noble) ambassadors, or rather lower-ranking (non-noble) envoys, ministers and minister-plenipotentiaries. Other lesser states had to be content with residents and secretaries. Some attempts were made to train young men for the diplomatic service. Peter the Great at the time of the Great Northern War, and Catherine II in 1779 tried a kind of apprenticeship scheme in Russia, and something rather similar was introduced in France in 1712. There young men were set to study documents relating to past negotiations of all kinds, in the hope that from them they would learn the principles of diplomacy. But diplomats usually received no training. If they had, it would have been of little practical value to them, for there was no career structure, and few prospects of promotion. All the top posts were automatically reserved for wealthy aristocrats, whose training as potential ambassadors was restricted to a first posting as secretary to a reasonably experienced senior diplomat in one of the major cities.

By the eighteenth century the tradition that diplomats should be paid by the state to which they were accredited had died out (except in the Ottoman Empire which still sometimes observed the earlier practice). Instead, diplomats' salaries became the reponsibility of the state which they represented. Ambassadors needed to be rich, for over and above their salary, they were expected to spend lavishly out of their own pockets in the service of their government and the maintenance of national prestige. In Poland in the 1760s, Russian and other diplomats spent enormous sums of money, much of it their own, to build up rival political factions among the *szlachta*. Difficulties sometimes arose if the ambassador's money ran out – the British ambassador was stranded in Poland after the Third Partition (1795) because the British government would not meet his expenses (see page 109). Diplomacy for an ambassador, in eighteenth century terms, was mainly a matter of representing his sovereign to another sovereign as elegantly as possible. To do that it was enough just to be a wealthy aristocrat, who, by meeting the right people socially, could make useful contacts and perhaps obtain from the gossip he heard some useful information to send back home. Little else was demanded of him, for the work of negotiation and details of agreements and so on would be dealt with by members of his household, often numbering 100 or more.

However, an ambassador was expected to fulfil one important duty – that of establishing and maintaining his state's diplomatic precedence: its position in the international pecking order. Each had to ensure that no slight was offered to his sovereign by any infringement of the precedence claimed and enjoyed by his representative. Numerous books of protocol were published, and widely read, for 'Points of honour, rank, precedence, are the most delicate aspects of political life.' The assumption of the title of King *in* (later *of*) Prussia by Frederick I in 1701, and of Emperor of Russia by Peter the Great in 1721 seriously upset the established order and caused grave offence to other states. As the eighteenth century progressed disputes about precedence declined in number and significance, although the niceties of protocol continued to exercise the minds of diplomats of all ranks until the end of the century.

e) Foreign Offices

By 1700 most states were beginning to develop some sort of centralised 'foreign office', divided into a number of departments, the whole under the guidance of a chief minister who often had substantial powers. Again, the pattern was set by France in the last years of Louis XIV's reign. By the early years of the eighteenth century the work of the already efficient French Foreign Office was greatly extended and elaborated. Specialised departments were set up: first a new official archive and a press bureau, then bureaux to look after the finest collection of maps in Europe, to deal with foreign despatches, to supervise finance and to conduct all current diplomatic business. The developments in France were matched by those in Russia, where the *Posolskii Prikaz* in 1705 was already one of the largest Foreign Offices in Europe, with 40 translators on its staff. It was replaced in 1719 by the College of Foreign Affairs, which, unlike its French counterpart, managed to shed other administrative and fiscal responsibilities with which it was burdened, and became concerned solely with foreign affairs.

While no other foreign offices expanded quite so rapidly as these two, in almost every European capital arrangements for the conduct of foreign policy became ever more complex and expensive as the number of diplomats and the extent of their activities increased. By the end of the eighteenth century, European diplomatic services had become efficient and homogenous institutions effectively controlled by their state governments. However, it was only the execution of foreign policy which was in the hands of foreign office officials. The formulation of that policy normally remained in the hands of the sovereign, who might or might not take ministerial advice, or indeed might not even seek it. Most sovereigns would have agreed with Catherine II, that foreign policy-making was the true *metier du roi*.

2 *Raison d'état*

The eighteenth century saw a change in the motives behind the foreign policy of Europe's rulers. In the sixteenth and seventeenth centuries religious and dynastic matters had been the most important. In the eighteenth century religion played no serious part in determining international policies among the major powers. However, it was sometimes made use of for propaganda purposes, as in Poland to justify aggression by Russia and Prussia in alleged support of the 'Dissidents' in the lead up to the First Partition (see page 69). Dynastic affairs – their names enshrined in the wars of the Spanish Succession, the Austrian Succession and the Polish Succession – continued to be important in the first half of the eighteenth century, but they were to become less so, as other grounds were found for territorial aggrandisment.

By the late eighteenth century international relations were conditioned by the doctrine of *'raison d'état'* (reason of state). This was the argument that the needs of the state dictated the political actions of its rulers. To do whatever was necessary to further self-interest became the right course of action for any ruler. Once this idea was generally accepted, it resulted in a competitive state system in Europe. In an age which rated states in accordance with the extent of their territory and the number of their people, the struggle for supremacy inevitably meant a new emphasis on military power. The possession of a large and successful standing army became the surest diplomatic weapon, for, in the words of Frederick II, 'in the end everything depends on power' and 'negotiations without arms produce as little impression as a musical score without instruments'. Might was equated with right, as rulers sought to add to their territories and increase their subject population, who in turn provided more revenue to support a larger army and acquire more territory. The whole basis of international relations in the eighteenth century was the idea of expansion – small states might be happy states, but they would be poor states; poor states were inevitably weak states and weak states were unlikely to survive. The ultimate extension of this thesis was that such states did not deserve to survive.

The practitioner *par excellence* of *raison d'état* was Frederick II of Prussia. When he invaded Silesia in December 1740, it was not only an act of unprovoked agression. It was also in direct contravention of his agreement to the Pragmatic Sanction, guaranteeing the peaceful succession of Maria Theresa to the Habsburg lands – an agreement which he had repeatedly assured the new Empress he intended to keep. Only five months earlier Frederick had published his pamphlet

The Anti-Machiavel. In it he had vehemently denounced the political theories of Machiavelli, which put the good of the state before anything else. His attack on Silesia was a complete denial of the moral stance which he had adopted previously. In a few short months he had become the most Machiavellian of all eighteenth-century monarchs, who could write:

1 There is only one good, that of the state itself . . . If we can gain something by being honest we will be honest, if we have to deceive, we will be cheats . . .

The nineteenth-century historian, Macaulay, described in scathing terms 'the selfish rapacity of the King of Prussia' in seizing Silesia, which eventually 'led the whole world to spring to arms. On the head of Frederick is all the blood which was shed . . .'. Many modern historians see Frederick's invasion of Silesia as the great turning-point in eighteenth-century international relations. Although it may, or may not, have 'ushered in a new era of international immorality', as one historian has claimed, it certainly marked a breach with the normally accepted order of treaty obligations, and set a precedent in territorial aggrandisement for others to follow. The loss of Silesia was to influence Austria's foreign policy for many years. When any hope of recovering Silesia had to be abandoned, Joseph II looked for compensation elsewhere, in Poland, in the Ottoman Empire and in Bavaria (see page 136).

By the second half of the eighteenth century the foreign policy of all major and of many minor European states was focused on the acquisition of additional territory, by peaceful negotiation if possible, by force if necessary. In those states which did not pursue this course of action, there was often what has been described as a 'stagnant' domestic policy where, for different reasons, innovations were not acceptable. States of this kind, such as Poland and the Ottoman Empire, tended to get left behind in the power game, for an inactive domestic policy seems to have been reflected in a non-aggressive foreign policy. Military power depended on economic strength. This in turn was dependent on the way in which the state's resources were exploited by the ruler. 'A well-conducted government must have a system as coherent as a system of philosophy . . . for the consolidation of the state and the increase of its power.'

3 The Balance of Power

One restraining element prevented violence becoming the only means of international communication. This was the concept of the balance of power. It was not a new idea, having first appeared in Italy in the late fifteenth century where it was used to prevent Venice from dominating the other city states. In the sixteenth and seventeenth centuries the 'balance of power' had been related to localised struggles, again in Italy, and in the Baltic and Germany. The difference in the eighteenth century was that it came to have a much wider application to the whole of Europe.

The Treaty of Utrecht (1713) declared its intention 'to confirm the peace and tranquillity of the Christian world through a just equilibrium of power (which is the best and most secure foundation of mutual friendship and lasting agreement in every quarter)'. Preserving a balance, or 'equilibrium' of power meant that no one state, or alliance of states, could be allowed to become too powerful and thus a danger to the peace of Europe. If it did, then the other states would combine together to reduce its power.

This was not to prove quite as simple as it sounded. Previously, in the sixteenth and seventeenth centuries, there had been only two main elements to balance – France and the Habsburgs. Minor states had supported one side or the other in a changing pattern of alliances. At the beginning of the eighteenth century the balance was still envisaged as France, supported by Bourbon Spain and some German states, against the Austrian Habsburgs, usually supported by Britain and the United Provinces. After 1713 no one state had the dominance over western Europe which France had enjoyed under Louis XIV, and this left the political situation much more fluid. Several diplomatic events – the Anglo-French alliance of 1717 and the Austro-Spanish agreement of 1725 – showed that the old pattern was not immutable, and the arrival of new players in the power game (Russia and Prussia in particular) began to disturb traditional policies. In 1756 the established order was totally shattered by the 'Diplomatic Revolution' (see page 65).

By the mid-eighteenth century there were five major powers, France, Austria, Britain, Russia and Prussia, which were generally regarded after 1763 as being of near equality in power. Any gains by one of these states caused alarm among the others, who invoked 'the balance of power' to justify territorial aggrandisement of the kind practised in the partitions of Poland by Austria, Russia and Prussia between 1772 and 1795 (see Chapters 6, 7 and 8).

4 Partition Diplomacy

'Partition diplomacy', as it came to be known, meant that where one state could not be prevented from acquiring territory at the expense of a weaker neighbour, other adjoining states were entitled to make similar gains for themselves in order to maintain the existing balance of power. The cheapest and easiest way to do this was not to fight an expensive war against an equal in order to obtain a share of the spoils, but by prior agreement, to dismember jointly the unresisting body of a weaker neighbour. 'The struggle for the balance of power is, in effect, the struggle for power' as the author of *The Political State of Europe* wrote in 1750.

The whole process of partition was given a spurious morality through the use of treaties of cession, allowing the tender conscience of monarchs such as Maria-Theresa to be quietened. Thus she was able to announce 'I am not opposed to settlement of these affairs by negotiation, but never by force of arms'. By the end of the eighteenth century political theorists were arguing that a state could justifiably be compelled by other states to sacrifice territory to which it had legal right, in the interests of the common good. By extension, this argument was used to defend partition diplomacy, on the grounds that the common good was the preservation of peace by the maintenance of the balance of power.

There were some critics of the idea that only the balance of power could preserve peace. Most of their theories were based on the sixteenth-century ideas of Grotius, and involved a federation of European states bound together by a 'social contract' and controlled by a representative supra-national body. These ideas were taken further, and by the end of the eighteenth century proposals were being made for a European Senate to be elected to adjudicate in disputes between states. Such proposals came to nothing, for in the end the consensus of opinion was that a balance of power was the best means of maintaining peace in Europe.

Partition diplomacy was sometimes associated with so-called 'archival diplomacy'. This was the use of dubious claims to ancient rights to the land a state planned to seize – for instance, Russia's claims to Kievan Rus, Austria's to Spisz and Galicia and Prussia's to Silesia. Frederick II was at least an honest enough rogue to admit openly at the time that Prussia's claims to Silesia were of little value and provided no justification for his invasion.

The precedent set by the First Partition of Poland made unilateral gains of territory, however obtained, increasingly impossible to achieve after 1773. Joseph II's attempts to acquire Bavaria, in the war of the Bavarian Succession (1777–8) and six years later in negotiations to exchange the Netherlands for Bavaria, both met with strong opposition from Frederick II. This Prussian hostility was an expression of general unwillingness by all the major powers to allow any one of their number to make substantial unilateral gains and so disturb the delicate balance of power.

Only in the Balkans and the Black Sea region was the situation different. There the growing strength of Russia and the weakness of the Ottoman Empire after the Treaty of Kutchuk-Kainardji (1774) allowed Catherine considerable freedom of action (see page 137). The annexation of the Crimea in 1783 was a decisive unilateral gain by Russia which could only have been prevented by concerted action on the part of the other major powers. Given the then existing antagonisms between them, this did not happen.

5 The 'Diplomatic Revolution'

The unexpected alliance of traditional enemies, Austria and France, in 1756 came as a shock to the rest of Europe. It was a total departure from the established pattern of diplomatic alliances, and created such astonishment that it was named the 'Diplomatic Revolution'. It was brought about partly by increased tension between France and Britain over colonial rivalries, and partly by the extreme hatred felt by Austria and Russia for the rising state of Prussia. The alliance was largely engineered by the Austrian Chancellor, Kaunitz. Since 1748 he had believed 'Frederick II is the greatest, most dangerous and most irreconcilable enemy' of Austria. Prussia, not France, should, therefore, be made the main target of Austrian foreign policy with the prime aim of recovering Silesia. Austria should look to her old enemy, France, and to her 'natural ally', Russia, for support against Prussia. The Empress Maria Theresa agreed with him, 'because I grow ever more and more convinced that the welfare of my house depends on the recovery of Silesia'.

Austria in particular benefited from the new alliance for it removed threats from France in Italy and Germany, and possible danger from the long-standing French connection with Austria's neighbour, the Ottoman Empire. The signing of a Convention between Britain and Prussia not only encouraged France to make the alliance with Austria, but angered Russia. The result was to drive Russia into plans for an Austro-Russian attack on Prussia. This attack was pre-empted by the Prussian invasion of Saxony in August 1756 which began the Seven Years War.

The most important aspects of the Diplomatic Revolution were that it brought to an end ancient enmities and destroyed the 'Old System', the anti-French Grand Alliance of Britain, Austria and the Dutch Republic. It built on the foundations already laid by Frederick II in 1740 for the power struggle between Austria and Prussia for control of Germany, which was to last for more than a century. In addition it marked the beginning of a shift of political emphasis from the countries of western Europe to those of the east. In the 20 years after the end of the Seven Years War the involvement of Britain and France in European affairs declined – their interests were concentrated on developments overseas. The problems of Europe were the fate of Poland and the decline of the Ottoman Empire, the expansion of Russia and the growing enmity of Prussia and Austria.

The Diplomatic Revolution proved to be something of an exception in international relations. Alliances generally continued to be made on the traditional basis that 'the enemy of my enemy is my friend' – it was shared hostility to France which had kept the 'Old System' of alliances together throughout three wars, for instance. Many rulers and their ministers distrusted formal alliances, believing, as Frederick II of Prussia did, that 'policy lies in profiting from favourable events, rather than preparing for them in advance . . . when [our people] are endangered by an alliance, our duty is to break it'. There was little room for idealism in foreign policy in the eighteenth century – success came to the strong and to the unscrupulous. Even one of the most high-minded statesmen of the 1740s had to admit:

1 a state should always be at the ready, living like a gentleman among swashbucklers and quarrellers. Such are the nations of Europe, today more than ever; negotiations are only a continual struggle between men without principles, impudently aggressive
5 and ever greedy.

6 Diplomacy and the Enlightenment

Not surprisingly the *philosophes* of the Enlightenment criticised the diplomatic practices of the eighteenth century as selfish and aggressive. In any case, according to enlightened political beliefs the emphasis should have been on internal reform and not on foreign affairs. The 'primacy of foreign policy' they believed to be an outdated concept. There is little evidence that the Enlightenment had any significant effect on the foreign policy of any major power. Those statesmen who are said to have been influenced by its teachings were few, and showed little sign of it in their actions.

7 Conclusion

Is it true that international relations were more immoral and unscrupulous in the eighteenth century than previously? Was 'international law made a mockery' and were 'public ethics practically non-existent' as some historians have asserted? Wars could begin without any formal declaration – but that was not new. Treaties could be broken and obligations ignored – but they had been before. Secret diplomacy, bribery and corruption, the interception of despatches, invasion without warning, seizure of land from the weak – none of these things were peculiar to the eighteenth century. They had existed before and would exist long after.

Why then does the eighteenth century have the unenviable reputation of 'a new era of international immorality'? Was it not so much *what* was done, as *how* and *why* it was done that made the eighteenth century different? Territorial aggrandisement was completed with all due ceremony – treaties of cession, formal agreements and correct process of law – after violence had achieved the desired end. Naked aggression was wrapped in a cloak of legality and made acceptable. Rulers no longer fought for an ideal, however misguided, or for their faith and seldom even for personal glory. They fought for

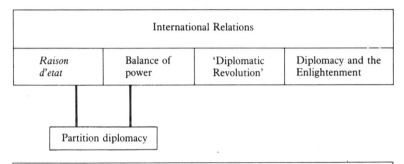

Diplomatic Organisation in the Eighteenth Century				
Immunity	Political espionage	Secret diplomacy	Training	Foreign offices

International Relations			
Raison d'etat	Balance of power	'Diplomatic Revolution'	Diplomacy and the Enlightenment

Partition diplomacy

Conclusion: The Character of Eighteenth Century Diplomacy?

Summary – Diplomacy in the Eighteenth Century

power. It is this calculating, cold-blooded cynicism which sets eighteenth-century diplomacy apart.

Making notes on 'Diplomacy in the Eighteenth Century'

This chapter deals with several different aspects of diplomacy in the eighteenth century. It begins with a straightforward account of the organisation and administrative practice of diplomacy at this time, and then goes on to look at the belief in *raison d'état* and the 'balance of power', which underlie the single most important diplomatic development of the eighteenth century – partition diplomacy. Understanding the nature of partition diplomacy, and how and why it was used, is the key to making sense of what happened in Poland and the Ottoman Empire after 1763.

The headings and sub-headings used in the chapter should help you to make your notes.

CHAPTER 6

The Partitions of Poland: The First Partition 1772–3

In the two decades after the end of the Seven Years War (1763), a new pattern of international relations was established in Europe. Attention was focused primarily on the east, where Russia, Prussia and Austria were occupied in making gains at the expense of their weaker neighbours.

1 Royal Election

The First Partition of Poland took place in 1773, but the troubles leading up to it had begun ten years earlier with the death of Augustus III. The prospects of a royal election provided Russia and Prussia with the opportunity to stage-manage events to their own advantage. As a first step they agreed to support a 'Piast' candidate (that is, a native born Pole). He would, they believed, be less likely to make difficulties for Poland's neighbours than a foreigner with pre-existing commitments. Frederick II's immediate concern was to prevent the election of Augustus's son, now the new Elector of Saxony, as King of Poland. The Saxons were serious rivals to Prussia in Germany, and an end to the Saxon-Polish link would obviously reduce Saxon power and prestige in the region, to the advantage of Prussia. Catherine II, too, did not wish to see a third Saxon king elected, as this would suggest that the Polish throne had become hereditary in the Wettin family. If that were so, all the opportunities for outside interference (which 'free' royal elections presented) would be lost. Only recently brought to power by a *coup d'état*, and somewhat insecurely established as Empress, Catherine was particularly anxious to ensure the security of her frontiers. In the west this was best, and most easily, done by maintaining the Russian hold on Poland which had existed since the beginning of the century. A compliant, Russian-sponsored, Piast king was needed. Catherine proposed Stanislaw Antoni Poniatowski. Frederick agreed to support her choice, provided, as he said, that Catherine 'made no noise' in arranging the election, and was careful not to provoke a war.

* Poniatowski, born in 1732, was, through his mother, one of the influential Czartoryskis who were known in Poland simply as the *Familia* – the family. He was well-educated and had travelled widely in western Europe, visiting Germany, Austria and Holland before arriving in England. There he found much to interest him, especially in the theatre and the arts, but also in the world of politics. After leaving London, he spent some time in Paris, before returning to

Poland at the age of 20. Fluent in six languages, cosmopolitan, intelligent and highly literate himself, he found the society of the Polish *szlachta* generally dull, provincial and stupid. In 1750 he stood for election to the *Sejm* and complained, 'For several days at the *sejmik* one had to talk nonsense with the rabble, express admiration for their ludicrous arguments, delight in their shallow concepts, and worst of all embrace their dirty, wretched persons'. In 1755 he was able to escape from his surroundings, going, as Polish minister-plenipotentiary to Russia, to stay with a friend, the newly-appointed British ambassador in St Petersburg, Sir Charles Hanbury-Williams. This visit changed Poniatowski's life, for there he was introduced by Sir Charles to the young Grand Duchess Catherine, whose official lover he quickly became. Other lovers took his place, and he returned home to Poland in 1758. He and Catherine did not meet again face to face for 30 years, but for all that time, and for ten years afterwards, their lives remained closely intertwined.

Catherine, concerned at the possibility of French opposition or of Ottoman intervention, needed foreign support to ensure Poniatowski's election. In 1733 Austria had been Russia's partner in manipulating the royal election, but in 1763 Austria was exhausted after the Seven Years War. Catherine therefore turned to Prussia. She was, after all, the daughter of a Prussian Field Marshal, who had served Frederick II. Frederick also was concerned about his state's security, although his worries were centred on Russia. As he said, he 'feared [Russia] more than he feared God'. By playing on Catherine's worries about the intentions of her other neighbour, the Ottoman Empire, he persuaded her to conclude a formal alliance with Prussia in 1764, based on an earlier treaty between Frederick and Tsar Peter III. The new alliance agreed that the two parties would ensure the election of Poniatowski, maintain Poland's 'Golden Freedom' (see page 15), and protect the rights of the Dissidents (Polish religious dissenters, both Lutheran and Orthodox). As a result of the success of the Counter Reformation in Poland, the country was fiercely Catholic – the Virgin Mary was not only Queen of Heaven, she was also Queen of Poland. Unfortunately tolerance had been turned into intolerance, and the comparatively small number of non-Catholics – Orthodox and Uniates in the east, and (mainly German) Lutherans in the north – were socially and politically disadvantaged and suffered some religious harrassment. Ever since the 'Tumult' of 1724 in the town of Thorn, when a minor confrontation between Lutherans and Catholics had led to riot, Prussia had been involved in a cynical exploitation of Dissident discontent.

* Rumours about the intentions of Prussia and Russia towards Poland quickly spread. Partition was mentioned as a possibility. Catherine was quick to disclaim any such idea:

1 If ever malice in concert with falsehood has been able to contrive

a completely baseless rumour, it is surely the one that we have resolved to support a Piast for one purpose only, namely that we could then easily invade several provinces of the realm of Poland,
5 dismember them and appropriate them forthwith to Ourselves and Our Empire. We have never had the intention, nor have we the need, to extend the limits of our Empire, which already consists of a large part of the globe.

However, it was not the first time that such rumours had circulated in Europe. In 1720 and again in 1733 Prussia had been involved in abortive plans for dismembering Poland. The Polish King, Augustus II, at one time talked of auctioning off part of the Republic among his neighbours. He even made overtures to the then King of Prussia with an offer of West Poland. The scheme came to nothing because of the death of Augustus II, but Frederick, who was only a young man at the time, seems to have kept it in mind. When in 1752 he was writing that Poland was like an artichoke, 'ready to be consumed, leaf by leaf', Prussia had still not been consolidated into a territorial entity. Her possessions were scattered across northern Germany. The two largest parts, Brandenburg and (Ducal) East Prussia were separated from each other by the substantial area of (Royal or Polish) West Prussia (see map on page 96). Here was a tempting artichoke leaf. However, like Catherine, Frederick was quick to deny any territorial ambitions in 1764: 'I am sure that your Court', he said to the Austrian ambassador, 'is alarmed about the treaty, and that at Vienna it is believed that we have already decided on the partition of Poland. But you will see that the contrary is the case.'

The Convocation *Sejm* met in Warsaw in April 1764 to make arrangements for the royal election. The problem of the Saxon candidate had solved itself; the new Elector had died suddenly of small-pox at the end of 1763, an event ascribed by Catherine to divine favour. He left only a 13-year-old son, and no other suitable Saxon contender could be found. A rival Piast candidate to Poniatowski was then put forward by the Branicki family. However, he was speedily put to flight together with his supporters, by a Russian army whose presence had been requested by Poniatowski's own family, the Czartoryskis. A group of Polish nobles at once wrote to Catherine to thank her for her help 'in defending Polish liberties'. The rival candidates having been disposed of, Poniatowski's victory was ensured by the expenditure in advance of large sums of Russian money and by the presence on the day of some 15,000 Russian troops on the election Field. Threats of force had the desired effect on the voters. On 6 September 1764 the new king was unanimously acclaimed in 'the quietest election' in the country's history, and took the name Stanislaw II August. More commonly known in the west as Stanislas-Augustus, he was to be the last King of Poland. His reign spanned

Stanislas–Augustus

exactly the years of the Partitions, 1764–95. Catherine spoke openly of 'the King we have made', and sent him 100,000 ducats. It was reasonable for her to suppose that he would do what he was told. Prince Repnin, the Russian government representative and agent in Warsaw, spoke for the Empress when he told Stanislas-Augustus, 'I am your master; you can only retain your crown by submission to me'. Despite this, it seemed for a time that with the election of Stanislas-Augustus a new era had begun in Poland.

* In the early days of his reign, he surprised everyone with his reforming zeal (as later he was to surprise them with his patriotism, however ineffective it proved to be). His efforts at reform soon brought him into conflict, first with his own relatives, the *Familia*, who found his ideas too radical for their taste, and then with Frederick II. The quarrel with Frederick illustrates one of the abiding problems of Poland. Whenever the Poles tried to introduce any sort of reform, political or economic, Prussia and/or Russia stepped in to prevent it becoming effective. In 1764, when the Convocation *Sejm* appointed a commission to organise a general customs system of the kind already operating elsewhere in Europe, Frederick immediately intervened. He built a fort on his side of the River Vistula from which he harassed and bombarded Polish trading ships, until the new proposals were abandoned. Poland had to be kept helpless, and under her neighbours' control. Then, no threat to anyone, she would continue to fulfil the function of a battleground on which her neighbours could settle their quarrels, peacefully or otherwise.

The Convocation *Sejm* was, as usual, confederated (that is, voting was by a majority). In 1765, under the Marshalcy of Stanislas-Augustus's cousin, it passed a number of important reform measures. Majority voting was made mandatory at *sejmiks* – a step towards the abolition of the *liberum veto* in the *Sejm*. Financial and military commissions were established, while other measures included a project for municipal reforms. Stanislas-Augustus put into effect some proposals of his own, including the creation of a new state-run military academy. Among those in the first intake of pupils was Tadeusz Kosciuszko, who was to become famous as a patriot and commander of the rebel army at the time of the Third Partition (see page 103).

2 The Dissidents

The following year, 1766, the first ordinary *Sejm* of the reign was presented with a major proposal for constitutional reform, the abolition of the *liberum veto*. To no one's surprise, considering the vested interests of the deputies, it was rejected. No progress was made either in improving relations between the Catholic Church and the Dissidents. The *Sejm* reaffirmed the situation which had existed since 1717, by which Dissidents were deprived of full political and civil rights and were excluded from holding government office. Their continued plight presented an ideal pretext for intervention – by Russia in support of the Orthodox, and by Prussia in support of the Lutherans – in accordance with the terms of the 1764 Russo-Prussian alliance. The Lutheran Frederick described himself as following a tolerant religious policy at home: 'I am neutral between Geneva and Rome', he wrote. 'By preaching moderation to all parties I strive to unite them.' But he was fully aware of the difficulties of interfering in the delicate matter of the Dissidents in Poland. After all, as he pointed out:

1 What would the Russian minister say if France were to invade
  Holland in order to force the Estates General to admit Papists to
  office? Would he not say that France was the aggressor? Apply
  this to the present situation in Poland . . . and it is the Russians
5 who are the aggressors . . .

For Catherine such niceties were irrelevant. She had been brought up as a Lutheran, and had converted to Orthodoxy on her marriage. By her own admission she had no great depths of religious belief. She certainly had no understanding of the strength of feeling in Catholic Poland against non-Catholics there. With total insensitivity she embarked on a programme of coercion. Repnin was sent to inform the *Sejm* of Catherine's demands. He deeply offended the deputies by speaking in Russian while remaining seated, and, worse still, while wearing his hat. The *Sejm* referred the whole matter to a committee of bishops, who did agree to introduce a number of minor changes to improve the position of the Dissidents.

Stanislas-Augustus was sympathetic to the plight of the Dissidents, but before he or the bishops could put any changes into effect, the country erupted into near civil war early in 1767. Two armed Confederations of Dissidents appeared – a Protestant one at Thorn and an Orthodox one at Slupsk. Neither Confederation was notable for its religious character, and both were in fact stage-managed by Repnin. At Thorn the Confederation was actually organised by a Russian officer, who began operations by arresting everyone, including the town council, who 'opposed the will of the Empress'. Repnin had to tread carefully at this point in order to prevent either Confederation gaining victory. Protestantism must not be allowed to spread too far in Poland, because 'it might, by limiting superstition and the power of the priesthood, rouse some Poles from their uncouthness'. This might encourage political reforms of the kind feared by Russia. Equally, though, the status of Repnin's fellow-Orthodox must not be made so secure that they no longer needed Russian protection. These Confederations were, for Repnin, simply a means of stirring up widespread unrest, a demonstration of the depths of 'Polish Anarchy' for all Europe to see. They were not intended to achieve anything else. Before the end of 1767 another, and much more important, General Confederation emerged, which quickly spread throughout the Republic.

Apart from its opposition to both Russia and Prussia, the aims of this General Confederation were far from clear. Its 80,000 or so members were of all shades of opinion. They included those who supported the King and those who wished to dethrone him, as well as those who merely wanted to stop his attempts at reform; those who believed the Catholic Church was in danger from Dissidents and those who wanted to see religious freedom for all. Under Russian pressure, an extraordinary meeting of the *Sejm* was called for the autumn to deal with the unrest.

Catherine's programme of coercion was gathering speed. The use of Russian money and troops ensured that the 'right kind' of deputies were elected to the *Sejm*. At its first meeting it received a note from Repnin announcing that he had arrested and sent as prisoners to Kaluga, just over the Russian border, four leading Catholic opponents of his policies. These included the Bishops of Cracow and Kiev, 'whose behaviour, by impugning the purity of Her salutary, disinterested and loving intentions towards the Republic, has insulted the dignity of Her Imperial Majesty, my Sovereign, the friend and ally of the Republic'. He warned that any further resistance to Russian demands for equality for the Dissidents would mean the deportation not of four, as in case of the bishops, but of 40 deputies. Pro-Russian deputies then suspended the sitting, and a special commission was appointed to negotiate with Repnin.

* The commission gave way – it had little alternative – and drew up the so-called 'Cardinal Laws'. These 'Five Eternal and Inviolable Principles', which were meekly accepted by the reconvened *Sejm* in February 1768, confirmed the nobility in their monopoly of political rights, agreed that royal elections should be 'free', and retained the 'Right of Resistance', the *liberum veto* and the landowner's power of life and death over his peasants. In addition, the Dissidents were granted freedom of worship, the right to build churches and to hold public office. A Perpetual Treaty with Russia embodied these Laws or Principles, and rehearsed how, 'at the request of the Polish 'Republic', Catherine 'extended a solemn guarantee for all time to maintain the constitution, form of government, freedoms and laws of Poland'. The two countries additionally guaranteed each other's territorial integrity.

It was a very satisfactory situation for Catherine. She had staked her reputation on obtaining redress for the Dissidents, and won. No Catholic power had thought it necessary to intervene in support of their Polish co-religionists. Poland was more firmly than ever under Russian control, and the constitution inviolate 'for all time'. She was well aware of the value of the *liberum veto* in obstructing reform, and the importance of retaining it. As she wrote to Repnin, nothing that the Poles did mattered, 'as long as we have the means of using the *liberum veto* when we need to.' 'Polish Anarchy' was safe in her hands.

3 The Confederation of Bar

A number of nobles had been disillusioned by the proceedings of the *Sejm*, and they rejected the legality of its decisions and of the treaty with Russia, as made under duress. They were angry, too, at the violent behaviour of the Russian troops still stationed in Poland despite Catherine's promises that they would be withdrawn. On 29 February 1768 a new Confederation of nobles was formed at Bar in Podolia, with the aim of defending the Catholic faith and driving the Russians out of Poland. A guerilla-type war was begun by the Confederates against both the Russians and the King and his government The war was to last for four years.

A provisional government set up by the Confederates announced the 'dethronement' of Stanislas-Augustus. A bungled attempt was made to kidnap him. He was snatched from his carriage in the middle of Warsaw, but the kidnap party soon afterwards lost its way. One of its members then had second thoughts about what they were doing and allowed the King to escape. He was back in his palace in Warsaw the next day, none the worse for his adventure, but the credibility of the Confederates was badly damaged as a result of the affair. However, they continued to receive financial support and the assistance of military advisers from France, which was at this time trying to form a Franco-Austrian-Saxon-Ottoman alliance to curb the activities of Russia and Prussia in eastern Europe.

The Confederate leaders' high-minded ideals and nationalist fervour, though, were not always understood by their fellow-countrymen. The mainly Orthodox peasants and Cossacks of the Ukraine embarked on a ghastly orgy of killing in a revolt aimed at nobles, Catholic priests and Jews. In three weeks of July 1768, nearly 200,000 people were killed before the rebels themselves were suppressed with equal brutality. Some groups of Cossacks, in pursuit of their quarry, crossed into Ottoman territory, where they attacked the town of Balta. This resulted in Russian troops being sent in large numbers to the Polish-Ottoman border area, to the consternation of the Ottoman government, which thought that the Russian army had been sent home. Further incursions into Ottoman territory by Russian and government troops pursuing Polish Confederates led to an Ottoman declaration of war against Russia in October 1768 (see page 132). Ottoman war aims included, among other things, Russian withdrawal from Poland, an end to the Russian guarantee of the Polish constitution and an end to Russian protection for Dissidents. The outbreak of war against the Ottomans was a severe blow to

Catherine. It necessarily diverted Russian troops from Poland, leaving the Confederates with the upper hand there.

General popular risings had already occurred in Cracow, in Wielkopolska (Great Poland) and in Lithuania during 1768. Travel conditions became so bad within the Republic by the end of that summer that only 30 deputies managed to attend the *Sejm* held in October. Russia warned that continued civil war might prove disastrous to Poland, by provoking further outside interference:

1 Not only Russia was interested in the dissidents but all Protestant powers, and if Catholic powers should meddle, then a war will follow, during which Catholicism may be completely exterminated in Poland.

The Poles took little heed, and fighting continued until August 1772, when the Russians finally overcame the last centres of resistance around Cracow. The magnates who had joined the Confederation went into exile, but over 5000 captured *szlachta* were deported to Siberia.

Two years later, in 1774, the war between Russia and the Ottoman Empire also came to an end. In it Russia had been spectacularly successful (see page 135). A peace settlement was finally made after lengthy negotiations initiated by Prussia and Austria, neither of whom wished to see Russia as outright winner. Too many Russian gains or too many Ottoman losses would have upset the balance of power in eastern Europe.

4 Plans for Partition

While the Russo-Ottoman war was still in progress, Frederick II had been considering how to make best use of the continuing confusion in Poland, and of Russian military commitments elsewhere, to further his own plans for acquiring West Prussia. He wrote in 1768:

1 It seems that the great obstacle will come from Russia. It will be better perhaps to acquire this province, bit by bit, by negotiation, rather than by conquest. On an occasion when Russia needs our assistance it will be possible to obtain what we want.

A few months later, at the beginning of 1769, he observed in a letter to his brother, Prince Henry:

1 Two courses are open to us; either to stop Russia in her pursuit of immense conquests, or, what will be the wisest, to endeavour

by good management to draw advantage from it. What could Austria do? She would be compelled either to take the part of
5 the Turks and Poles, or she would be seduced by Russia, who would offer her a piece of the cake. Prussia in such a case would find herself between Austria and Russia. To make our way out of this dilemma it will be necessary to indemnify Russia for the costs of her war with the Ottoman Empire, to separate Austria
10 from France, and to satisfy Austria in such a way as to remove the temptations to her of an alliance with Russia.

As the war progressed French and Austrian opposition to Russian expansion in the Balkans increased. If either of these countries entered the war on the side of the Ottomans it would activate the two main

The Royal Cake

defensive alliances of the period, between France and Austria and between Russia and Prussia. This might well precipitate a general European war. Frederick II's scheme for preventing such a war, and for bringing the existing war to an end, was an extension of the ideas he had expressed earlier to his brother; a tripartite partition of Poland, in which Russia and Austria would participate along with Prussia. Peaceful gains in Poland would be preferable to general war – for all, that is, except the Poles, who were not consulted – and much better than allowing Russia to make large unilateral gains from the Ottoman Empire, thereby upsetting the balance of power in eastern Europe to the disadvantage of Prussia and Austria.

It is not clear whether this particular scheme for a partition of Poland was Frederick's, or was based on one put forward by a retired Danish diplomat. On balance it seems probable that it was Frederick's own idea; he had certainly been toying with something similar for a considerable time. He wrote to his ambassador in St Petersburg, instructing him to approach Catherine with certain proposals. These were that Russia should offer some suitable part of Poland to Austria, in return for Austrian military assistance against the Ottomans; Prussia should be given West Prussia, the province of Wormie, and suzerainty over Danzig, in return for the substantial war subsidies which Prussia had provided to Russia under the terms of the Russo-Prussian treaty of 1764; while Russia should take as compensation to cover her war expenses, and as recompense for 'what she had refrained from acquiring' from the Ottomans, whatever part of Poland seemed appropriate. Frederick added:

> 1 If Austria gets no part of Poland, all the hatred of the Poles will
>   be turned against us. They would regard the Austrians as their
>   protectors, and the latter would win so much prestige and influ-
>   ence with them, that they would gain thousands of opportunities
> 5 for intrigue of all kinds in the country.

The Prussian ambassador doubted whether the proposals would be acceptable to the Russian government but he finally broached the subject with the Russian Foreign Minister, who was not enthusiastic. However, Catherine did not reject the plan out of hand. Frederick encouraged her acceptance of the idea by pointing out how kind she had always been to the unworthy Poles, how they had spurned her kindness, and how little they deserved her consideration. Frederick's principal advocate of Prussian expansion at the expense of Poland was his brother, Prince Henry, who visited the Russian court at the end of 1770. In January 1771 Catherine made it clear to him that she would not object in principle to a partition of Poland. However, this decision was due to factors other than Prussian urgings. The Poles had disappointed her by their lack of docility under Russian control; more draconian measures were necessary to bring them to their senses. In addition, the cost of the war against the Ottomans was heavy, there was no guarantee that territorial gains made in the Crimea could be retained, and there was disquieting news that a secret defensive treaty was being made between the Ottomans and Austria, whose access to the Black Sea coast was threatened by Russian advances in the south. It would be easiest for Russia to fall in with the Prussian plan and to seek agreed compensation in Poland for her war expenses, rather than in the Ottoman Empire, where her gains by conquest might not be permanent.

* In a memorandum of this time Frederick cynically expressed his views:

1 Assuming that Russia is resolved to compensate herself in Poland for her immense outlay in the Turkish war, it remains to examine the most suitable moment to apply the plan. I think we must reject the notion for an arrangement with the Court of Vienna.
5 Why? because it is ill-disposed to the Russian court and Prince Kaunitz [Austrian chief minister] . . . likes to humiliate those who make such proposals. I have too much self-respect to submit to his judgement, and I do not suppose that anyone in Russia would advise the Empress [Catherine] to submit to his whims, as
10 if we could not occupy the territories we need without his approbation and investiture. On the contrary, I think we should imitate the conduct of the Court of Vienna, which, without prior consultation or permission, occupied certain districts. As for the Poles, when we occupy our respective portions they will doubtless raise
15 shrill cries, as this vain and insolent nation always does . . .

The 'certain districts' to which Frederick referred were lands around Spisz (Zips) and three other places on the Austrian-Hungarian border. Austria laid claim to these on the very dubious grounds that they had once, 300 years earlier, been part of the crown lands of Hungary. In 1769 Austria had invaded and subsequently annexed these areas to form a barrier which was intended to prevent the war in Poland from spilling over into Habsburg territories, for the possession of Spisz closed the one gap in the mountainous frontier with Poland. Using the excuse that plague was sweeping Europe, and that to prevent its spread it was necessary to set up a buffer zone, or what he preferred to call a *cordon sanitaire*, Frederick followed the Austrian example and seized a border area of Poland. Precedents had been set for bigger and better seizures of Polish territory in the future.

In his *Memoirs*, Frederick ascribes much of the delay in putting the partition proposals into effect to 'the slowness and irresolution of the Russians'. He adds,

1 The negotiations hung chiefly on the possession of the city of

Danzig. The Russians pretended that they guaranteed the liberty
of this little Republic; but it was the English who, jealous of the
Prussians, protected this maritime town and prompted the
5 Empress of Russia not to consent to the demands of the Prussian
Majesty . . . As it was evident that the mastery of the Vistula
would in time subject that city, the King [of Prussia] decided it
was not necessary to stop such important negotiations, for an
advantage which could only be deferred; therefore his Majesty
10 relaxed the demand . . . After so many obstacles had been
removed the secret contract was signed at St Petersburg in
February, 1772 . . . and it was agreed that the Empress-Queen
[Maria-Theresa] should be invited to join the two contracting
parties and partake of the partition.

Memoirs are notoriously unreliable historical sources. Often written
long after the event, and frequently reworked to show the author in a
more favourable light than was justified by events, they need to be
used with care. Much that Frederick wrote in his *Memoirs* and in his
political testaments is suspect, involving a good deal of wishful
thinking, and elements of 'being wise after the event'. It is not easy to
disentangle truth from fiction in any autobiographical writing –
Catherine the Great was as adept at self-deception (see page 33) as
Frederick. Primary sources contemporary with the events with which
they are concerned – letters, memoranda, speeches, interviews and
conversations – are more likely to be reliable, but even these need to
be evaluated carefully by the historian. The evidence they provide
cannot always be taken at its face value, for much depends on the
intention of their authors at the time they were written.
  * When Maria-Theresa of Austria was first approached by
Frederick with the idea of partition, she was less than enthusiastic.
She wrote to her chief minister, Kaunitz:

1 I do not understand the political system which, in the case where
  two Powers make use of their superiority to oppress an innocent
  opponent, allows a third to imitate and follow their example. A
  prince has no rights other than a private person. The greatness
  and the maintenance of his state will not enter into the matter
5 when he shall have to render account of what he has done . . .
  Let us pass for feeble rather than dishonest. Let us attempt to
  reduce the pretensions of these others rather than join them in a
  partition so unequal.

Maria-Theresa's scruples over the proposed partition appear
hypocritical in view of Austria's earlier seizure of the border areas
around Spisz. Early in 1772, Maria-Theresa was formally presented
with the terms of the convention signed in St Petersburg which stated

that the Empress of Russia and the King of Prussia 'considering the general confusion in which the Republic of Poland exists by the dissension of its leading men, and the perversity of all its citizens', declared the need to unite parts of that country to their own states. They promised to support one another against any opposition, and invited the Empress of Austria to join with them. Kaunitz and Maria-Theresa had both been opposed to the idea of a tripartite partition – Kaunitz because not only Austria but Russia and, worse, Prussia would benefit as well, and Maria Theresa because she still regarded the idea of partition as a crime. But political logic dictated that Austria could not stand by while Russia and Prussia benefited without her. Kaunitz accordingly gave in, and accepted the inevitability of partition. Maria-Theresa, pressured by her son Joseph as well as by Kaunitz, eventually and with great reluctance also agreed:

1 since so many learned men will have it so, but, long after I am dead, it will be known what this violation of all that we have hitherto held sacred and just gives rise to.

5 The First Partition

In August 1772 (the same month in which the Confederates of Bar were finally defeated and their war with Russia came to an end) the Treaties of Partition were signed in St Petersburg. The preamble stated that:

1 The spirit of faction, the troubles and internal war which has shaken the kingdom of Poland for so many years and the Anarchy which gains new strength every day . . . give just apprehension for expecting the total decomposition of the state . . . at the same time
5 the Powers neighbouring on the Republic are bur-dened with rights and claims which are as ancient as they are legitimate . . .

Russian ministers had already pointed out that their moderation in claiming less than they were entitled to was 'a pledge which Russia advances for the solidity of peace'. Austrian pronouncements were in much the same vein, while Prussia went further:

1 We trust that the Polish nation will eventually recover from its prejudices, that it will acknowledge the enormous injustice which it has done to the House of Brandenburg, and that it will bring itself to repair it by a just and honourable arrangement.

Following these individual self-justifications the three powers issued a joint statement in September 1772 describing the unhappy condition

into which, in their view, Poland had sunk and from which she needed to
be rescued and her neighbours to be protected, lest worse befall:

1 The spirit of discord has seized upon one part of the nation and
  citizen has armed against citizen. Law, order and public safety,
  justice, commerce and agriculture, all are going to ruin or stand
  already on the brink of destruction.

They continued with a grim warning, which also contained a thinly
veiled threat:

1 Excesses of every kind, the consequence of such anarchy, will
  bring total dissolution on the state if not timely prevented.

The manifesto concluded with a statement of intent:

1 Having communicated their rights and claims, and being convinced of the justice thereof, they are determined . . . to take
  immediate and effectual possession of such parts of the territory
  of the Republic as may serve to fix more natural and sure bonds
5 between her and the three Powers.

These territorial 'rights and claims' were very suspect, relating as they
did to territories which had been Polish for the best part of two
centuries, and, in the case of Austria's claim to Galicia, for a great deal
longer. The claims were strongly contested by Stanislas-Augustus as
unjust. Indeed, their only purpose was to lend a semblance of legality
to an act of violence.
  Maria-Theresa, acting on behalf of the three powers, replied to
Stanislas-Augustus, expressing her 'unspeakable astonishment' at the
attitude which he was adopting, and adding that she hoped:

1 that the King of Poland will not expose his kingdom to events
  which must be the consequence of his delay to summon the *Sejm*,
  but will enter upon a negotiation which alone can save his country.

  * Stanislas-Augustus, his country full of foreign troops, was
persuaded by the new Russian ambassador to summon a *Sejm*. Before
it met, all that remained for the three powers to do was to agree
exactly how much territory to take, so that the partition treaties could
be drawn up ready for ratification. Something had to be left intact, for
as the Russian Foreign Minister was at pains to point out, 'Poland
must remain for ever as an intermediary state, destined to prevent a
collision between her three neighbours'. In the end, Prussia took

36,000 square kilometres with 580,000 inhabitants; Austria 83,000 square kilometres with 2,650,000 inhabitants and Russia 92,000 square kilometres with 1,300,000 inhabitants (see map on page 96). Prussia's share, although the smallest, was also the most valuable. It included the most developed areas and gave Prussia control of much of the important commercial waterway of the Vistula. It also provided the desired land bridge between East Prussia and the rest of the kingdom. Frederick's primary ambition had been realised.

A confederated *Sejm* met in April 1773. Its sole purpose was to confirm the partition treaties. Suitable and compliant deputies had been elected at *sejmiks* sweetened by foreign money, and surrounded by foreign troops. Only a very few members of the *Sejm* were prepared to oppose the ratification openly. One senator did resign his office. 'I would rather sit in a dungeon and cut off my hand than sign the sentence passed on my Fatherland', he wrote. 'A Pole who permits the partition of his country would be sinning against God.' Even more exceptional was a spectacular protest by Tadeusz Rejtan, a young and patriotic envoy. After begging his fellow members in an impassioned speech to reject the partition, he threw himself on the floor and, tearing his clothes, cried, 'On the blood of Christ, I adjure you, do not play the part of Judas; kill me, stamp on me, but do not kill the Fatherland.' It was to no avail. Prussia and Russia threatened to seize more territory if the Poles did not cooperate. In the summer of 1773 Stanislas-Augustus signed the necessary documents, and in September three separate treaties ceding territory to the partitioning powers were ratified by the *Sejm* without a vote being taken. The Marshal of the *Sejm* merely declared the treaties accepted. The First Partition was complete.

* The countries of western Europe had expressed little interest or concern in what was happening to Poland. Only one sovereign, the King of Spain, made an official protest. The British government was informed by Sir James Harris, the British minister in Warsaw, as early as March 1772, that a treaty of partition 'disposing of several parts of Poland' had already been signed in St Petersburg between Prussia and Russia. Three months later, in early June, Harris received a reply from London, expressing mild interest, and asking how 'the curious transaction' had been carried out. The letter added, ingenuously, 'We hear from Warsaw that the consternation in that Court on the subject of dismemberment is as great as it is natural to expect it would be.' So great indeed was the agitation in the Polish court, that Stanislas-Augustus wrote personally to King George III asking for British help to maintain the balance of power in eastern Europe and to restrain the activities of Prussia, Russia and Austria. Unhelpfully, George III replied:

1 For long I have seen with sorrow the evils which surround your Majesty, and which have ruined Poland. I fear that these misfortunes have reached such a point that they can only be redressed

by the Almighty – I can see no other intervention which could
5 be of any remedy.

6 Results of the First Partition

The most obvious result was that Poland lost some 30 per cent of her
territory and 35 per cent of her population, reducing the country to
about the same size as France. The loss of control over the Lower
Vistula, Poland's trade route to the Baltic coast and to the outside
world, was very serious. The situation was made worse by Prussia
taking advantage of the partition negotiations to extract a commercial
agreement from the Poles. This put extortionate duties on Polish corn
rafted down the river, with disastrous results for an already declining
trade. Although Poland had kept possession of Danzig, the loss of
West Prussia left the city isolated and unprotected.

Harris, now the British minister in Berlin and aware of growing
concern among British merchants over the future of Danzig, tried
again to persuade his government to intervene in Poland:

1 The dominion which his Prussian Majesty has over the councils
  of St Petersburg, and the infatuation with which everything is
  received there that comes from Potsdam, will, I am afraid, cause
  the Empress Catherine to listen with more attention to the insi-
5 dious language of the King of Prussia than it deserves, and
  entirely prevent her from taking any share with us for the preservation of the liberties of Danzig and commerce of Poland . . .

The British government once more disappointed Harris, making it
clear that it had no intention of doing anything to preserve the
liberties of Danzig. The only advice it gave was that the city should
make the best bargain it could with Frederick II to safeguard its
economy. 'I pity the poor city', wrote an English representative in
Danzig. 'Russia has betrayed it, and sold it ignominiously'.

* Historians from western Europe have almost universally condemned Frederick II for his part in bringing about the First Partition.
The plan was largely his – he needed West Prussia to consolidate his
existing territories, and he set out quite cynically to obtain it by
undisguised aggression. Catherine, at least initially, would have
preferred to retain the status quo with Poland as a Russian
protectorate. Frederick's persuasive powers, the Ottoman war and a
growing fear that if she did not agree to a tripartite partition, Prussia
might proceed to a unilateral annexation of part of Poland, so
provoking a war, combined to change her mind. Frederick at least had
the grace to realise that he and Catherine were 'simply brigands',
taking what they wanted without contrition. Even Maria-Theresa
'partook of the cake'. As Frederick unkindly, but correctly, said, 'the

more she cried, the more she took', leaving him 'to wonder how she squared her confessor'. The truth was that none of the three powers could afford to be at a disadvantage with respect to the others, if the balance of power was to be maintained.

★ Within Poland there were a large number of citizens who cooperated with the partitioning powers, usually for financial or other gain, like the dissolute priest appointed by Catherine as Archbishop and Primate of Poland. Some Poles, however, seem to have genuinely believed that the Russians were their true 'protectors'. So used were they to the Russian presence in their country that they were willing to cooperate, for good, if mistaken, reasons. Those prepared to risk life, career and family by open opposition were few and far between.

Opposition was difficult; change almost impossible. The Cardinal Laws (The Five Eternal Principles – see page 74) had been reaffirmed by the *Sejm* in 1773. Catherine swore to uphold the status quo within what remained of the Republic. Constitutional reform was impossible without her consent, and it was not in her interest to give it. While the 'Golden Freedom' continued, Poland would remain politically weak and at the mercy of her stronger neighbours. Nevertheless, the 1770s and 1780s saw a series of limited reforms introduced with Russian consent. The Russian party was strong enough to afford a few concessions which did not undermine the principles of the protectorate.

The executive powers of government were vested in 1775 in a Permanent Council, of which the King was the nominal head. The Council had five departments, or ministries, which began a series of administrative reforms to modernise government practice. The Treasury was made more efficient and the army was modernised – although, under the terms of the treaty with Russia, it could not be enlarged. The Police Department was made more effective, and the enforcement of law and order was more thoroughly managed. A Commission for National Education – in effect a ministry for education, the first of its kind in Europe – was set up by the King in 1774. Economic developments of all kinds, which had been begun before the First Partition, were continued. Manufacturing industries, especially textiles and ceramics were encouraged, more canals were dug and the postal service was extended. Banks were founded, and new trading companies were set up. Much of this activity was due to a direct interest taken by the King.

In 1773 the *Sejm* repealed the law forbidding the *szlachta* to engage in commerce. As a result, many of the magnates began to involve themselves in business enterprises. Most of these were small factories and workshops based on large estates and worked by peasant labour. Some magnates proved extremely enterprising. One of the Potocki family even operated a merchant fleet on the Black Sea and in the Mediterranean. Industrial development was mainly restricted to the countryside, and Warsaw was exceptional among Polish towns, not only for its size (150,000 in 1792), but for its large urban proleteriat. (They were to play an important part in the Rising of 1793–4). In 1776 the King commissioned a new Code of Laws, which was published in 1780. Although it was rejected by the *Sejm*, partly due to Prussian interference, it was an important document which laid the foundations of later reforms.

* Real authority still lay with the Russian ambassador, but by the 1780s Stanislas-Augustus had begun to move cautiously towards a more independent foreign policy. Opportunities for this were made possible by Catherine's fresh entanglements with Sweden and the Ottoman Empire. In 1787 Catherine was making a 'progress' through her newly acquired southern lands, partly by land and partly by water. When the imperial barge reached Kaniow on the River Dnieper, waiting for the Empress on the Polish bank was Stanislas-Augustus. It was their slightly embarrassing first meeting for 30 years. He had come to suggest a Russo-Polish defensive alliance against the Ottomans, by which Poland would receive Moldavia and a Black Sea port, as well as a share in the expected profits of Russia's Black Sea trade. In return, Poland (if Russia agreed to an increase in the Polish army) would provide substantial military assistance against the Ottomans and would also protect Russia from a backdoor attack through Poland by Prussia or Sweden. The meeting was not entirely harmonious – Catherine snubbed Stanislas-Augustus by refusing to go ashore to attend a ball which he had arranged for her. Nevertheless, Stanislas-Augustus expected to receive a positive reply in due course. On his return to Warsaw, confident of success, he summoned the *Sejm* to a special sitting, the sole purpose of which would be to ratify the new alliance.

But Catherine turned down the King's offer. In a private letter she wrote:

1 It is necessary to dismiss the personal concerns of the king and his ministers, and to keep the constitution as it is now. For truth to tell there is no need or benefit to Russia from Poland becoming more active.

The British minister in Warsaw in July 1788 was very aware of the difficult situation imposed upon the Republic:

1 Since the Partition, Poland possesses neither her own history nor a politically independent existence. Deprived of trade, having not a single external ally, possessing neither sufficient internal strength nor revenues enabling emancipation from foreign rule,
5 squeezed by three powerful monarchies on all sides, she seems to be waiting in silence for a sentence that will bring about her emptiness . . . This is the fate of a country which under clever

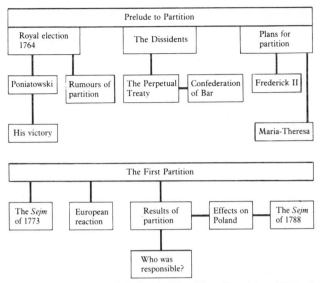

Summary – The Partitions of Poland: The First Partition 1772–3

management could easily rank among the first powers of Europe . . .

Unexpectedly, the *Sejm*, which had been summoned by Stanislas-Augustus solely to approve the projected Russo-Polish alliance, continued in session even after its statutory six weeks were up and it had become clear that no such alliance was to take place. Taking advantage of Catherine's continued distraction by the Ottoman war it began to pursue a programme of constitutional reform. In the four years between 1788 and 1792 the 'Great Sejm' destroyed the Russian protectorate, which had existed since 1717 – and thereby precipitated the death of the Republic.

Making notes on 'The Partitions of Poland: The First Partition 1772–3'

'The Partitions of Poland' is a very popular topic with examiners. You are, therefore, very likely at some stage to be faced with an essay question of the type discussed on page 130.

This and the next two chapters contain information which you will need for your answer, by providing (a) a chronological survey of the three partitions, (b) a consideration of the motives of Russia, Austria and Prussia, and (c) in Chapter 8, a discussion of who was to blame for the destruction of Poland.

The headings used throughout the chapter should help you make notes on the First Partition.

Source-based questions on 'The Partitions of Poland: The First Partition 1772–3'

1 Prussia and Austria

Read the remarks of Frederick II on Austrian participation in the partition of Poland on pages 76, 77 and 78. Answer the following:

a) Explain 'a piece of the cake' (page 77, line 6), and 'certain districts' (page 79, line 13). (2 marks)

b) In the first extract what does Frederick consider to be the threats which Austria presents to Prussia's international position, and how does he plan to counter them? (4 marks)

c) What is suggested is Frederick's opinion of (i) Austria, (ii) Russia, and (iii) Poland? Explain your answer. (6 marks)

Now read Maria-Theresa's views on partition (pages 80 and 81) and answer the following questions:

d) What are her objections to partition? On what grounds are they based? What is her excuse for finally agreeing to partition? (5 marks)

e) What impression of Maria-Theresa is given by these two extracts? Explain your answer. How far does it accord with what else you know of her? (8 marks)

2 The First Partition

Look at the engraving reproduced on the page 77 and read the extracts from the preamble to the treaty (page 81) and from the individual and joint statements issued by the three powers (pages 81 and 82). Answer the following questions:

a) Explain 'Anarchy' (page 81 line 2), 'rights and claims . . . as ancient as they are legitimate' (page 81, line 6), 'the enormous injustice to the House of Brandenburg' (page 81, line 3). (5 marks)

b) Explain the title of 'The Royal Cake' given to the engraving. Why is it usually described as a 'satirical' drawing? (3 marks)

c) How do the three powers justify their actions? (3 marks)

d) What attitude did the three powers adopt towards (i) Poland, and (ii) her king? How are these attitudes reflected in the engraving? (9 marks)

CHAPTER 7

The Partitions of Poland: The Second and Third Partitions 1793 and 1795

1 The Great *Sejm* 1788–92

In 1788 Prussia's Frederick William, who had succeeded Frederick the Great as king in 1786, put forward a proposal to acquire further land in Poland without fighting for it. His ideas, embodied in the Hertzberg plan, were complicated and required a series of exchanges – a not uncommon eighteenth-century diplomatic ploy. The Ottomans, who were at war with Russia and were about to be involved in war with Austria, should cede Moldavia and Wallachia to Austria; Austria should return Galicia to Poland, which in gratitude would cede Danzig and Thorn to Prussia. Russia would acquire Bessarabia and Ochakov (a fort at the mouth of the Dnieper) from the Ottomans, and in return Russia, Prussia and Austria would guarantee the integrity of Ottoman territory south of the Danube. The Emperor of Austria, Joseph II, opposed the plan, for he distrusted and feared Prussia. He concluded an agreement with Catherine II whereby she would support Austria against any effort by Prussia to acquire land in Poland by whatever means, direct or indirect.

Other foreigners also had an interest in Poland. The most notable of these was Count Potemkin, Catherine's long-time lover (some said husband), and one of her trusted advisers and army commanders. By various means he had acquired large estates in south-eastern Poland, with over 100,000 serfs. In 1788 he seems to have been plotting with Polish magnates to set up a national 'host', allegedly as a first step towards the proclamation of a new confederation to defend Poland against the Ottomans, maintain the Catholic faith and preserve the freedoms of the Polish *szlachta*. Some, however, suspected that his motives were not entirely disinterested. They distrusted his ambitions, believing, as his niece said, that he intended 'to win over all the Cossacks, unite with the Polish army and proclaim himself king of Poland', despite his Russian birth and Orthodox faith.

In Poland itself there had always been opposition to what seemed to be Stanislas-Augustus's pro-Russian attitude. His failure to bring the proposed Russo-Polish alliance to a successful conclusion in 1787–8 was a humiliation not only for his country but for him personally. He had long been interested in politics and in the possibility of constitutional reform in Poland; in 1788 his disillusionment with Catherine and with Russian policy pushed him into the arms of the reformers. A group of magnates, who had formed themselves into the 'Patriotic Party', began to plan how to end Russian influence in Poland. They were encouraged in their hopes by news of a Prussian alliance with the 'maritime powers', Britain and Holland, which was aimed at curbing further Russian expansion. With, it was hoped, a rather more friendly Prussia, and with Russia tied down by wars against the Ottoman Empire and Sweden, the time seemed propitious for reform.

The *Sejm* which met in October 1788 had been summoned for the sole purpose of agreeing the proposed Russo-Polish alliance (see page 86). When this alliance proved to be abortive, the *Sejm*, instead of dispersing after six weeks like all its predecessors, remained in session for the next four years. There was, in fact, another election of delegates at the end of two years, but these did not replace the earlier ones. They were simply added to the original members. For its last two years the *Sejm* had about 600 members, twice its usual size. As it was confederated, the *liberum veto* could not be used, and voting was by a simple majority.

From the early days of what came to be known as the 'Great *Sejm*' there was always the danger of Russian intervention in its affairs. But Catherine's preoccupation with war against the Ottomans made this less likely than would normally have been the case, and under the influence of the Patriotic Party the *Sejm* settled down to a programme of reform, without reference to Russia. It began by debating a number of measures aimed at strengthening national sovereignty and reviving the economy. These included the abolition of the Permanent Council set up in 1773, and a demand for the withdrawal of all Russian troops from the country. For the first time ever, a direct tax of ten per cent on income from *szlachta* lands and of twenty per cent on income from church lands was imposed. Plans were made to increase the size of the army which still stood at only 18,000. In 1789 the *Sejm* gave a sympathetic hearing to a deputation of burghers from 141 towns, asking for representation in government – the first crack in the *szlachta's* monopoly of government. So heavy did the pressure of business become, that in 1790 the *Sejm* divided itself into two chambers in order to speed up the process of decision-making.

The *Sejm* achieved what Stanislas-Augustus had failed to do, and successfully negotiated an independent foray into foreign policy in March 1790 with the conclusion of a Prusso-Polish treaty clearly aimed against Russia. Among the clauses was an undertaking by Prussia to assist Poland with an army of 18,000 men against any attempt by a foreign power to interfere in Polish internal affairs in the name of a previous guarantee of the Polish constitution.

a) The Constitution of 1791

Political debate, both inside and outside the *Sejm*, had been growing more radical each year. One of those most influential in forming political opinion was Hugo Kollataj, a priest, an intellectual and a powerful orator. He founded a pressure group, the Forge, whose members were articulate but pacific campaigners for what Kollataj described as 'a gentle revolution'. In 1788 he addressed the *Sejm*:

1 What then is Poland? It is a poor useless machine which cannot be worked by one man alone, which will not be worked by all men together, and which can be stopped by a single person.

He supported the enfranchisement of non-nobles, and was the author of the petition which representatives of the 141 towns presented to the King and the *Sejm*. In it he warned, 'The slave will violently tear his bonds asunder if his ruler stifles the Rights of Man and of the Citizen.' A year later, in 1790, he published *The Political Law of the Polish Nation*, which set out his programme for reform, and which formed the basis of the 1791 Constitution.

On 3 May 1791 the *Sejm* was the scene of a *coup d'état*, prepared by the Patriotic Party, with the assistance of the Marshal of the *Sejm* and with the knowledge and support of the King – perhaps it was even at his instigation. They chose a day when two thirds of the members were absent on the last day of the Easter holiday; of the 182 deputies present, 100 had been let into the secret. A report prepared in advance by the Committee on Foreign Affairs was presented to the *Sejm* by the Marshal. This pointed out the dangers of continued delay in carrying out the reform of the constitution. Turning to the King, the Marshal said, 'It is your duty, sire, to prepare measures which will provide means for saving the state.' A ready-made document was promptly produced by the King and read to the deputies. Its preamble proclaimed:

1 Freed from the shameful coercion of foreign orders and cogni-
 zant of the ancient faults of our system of government, and valu-
 ing national independence and freedom above life itself . . . We
 pass the following statute in recognition that the fate of us all
5 depends exclusively on the foundation and perfection of a
 national constitution . . .

Questions of a quorum were brushed aside. The bill was accepted by acclamation and the King signed the documents. The constitution had become law, the first written constitution in Europe. Outside in the square the soldiers and the crowd cried 'Long live the King! Long live the Constitution!' as the King and the deputies processed to the cathedral to swear to uphold the new constitution, and to sing a celebratory *Te Deum*. Poland had been transformed in the course of a day into a hereditary constitutional monarchy, and many causes of the country's internal weaknesses had been removed at a stroke.

The new constitution ended 'free' royal elections. The crown was to become hereditary. On the death of Stanislas-Augustus, who had no direct heir, the crown would pass to the Elector of Saxony and his heirs. The *liberum veto* was abolished and was replaced by majority voting. The 'Right of Resistance', enshrined in the custom of armed confederation, was abolished 'as contrary to the spirit of the constitution and as tending to trouble the state'. The power of the provincial *sejmiks* was reduced and the *Sejm* was to have two chambers. The executive was to be in the hands of 'the Guardians of the Laws', a group consisting of the King, the primate, and five ministers appointed by the King for a period of two years at a time. These Guardians were made directly answerable to the *Sejm*. The King was to remain in command of the army, now to consist of 100,000 men. Citizens of the towns were to have the same political privileges as the *szlachta*, and were to elect their own representatives to sit in the *Sejm*. However, the peasants were not to be represented, despite the wishes of many of the reformers. They were merely given what they were supposed to have had before, 'the protection of the law and government of the country'. A new, centrally-administered provincial government system was to be set up to replace existing local commissions, and the tax system was to be further revised. Roman Catholicism was to remain the national religion, but tolerance was to be shown to other groups. The message of the reformers was clear: 'all power in the state comes from the will of the nation'. Stanislas-Augustus himself, referring to possible repercussions from Russia, came out into the open on the side of reform, and said that any danger was preferable to the old state of dependency. 'In future the Poles are going to govern themselves' he declared. It was to prove an empty boast.

With the notable, but hardly unexpected exception of Russia, the new constitution was generally well received. The British minister in Warsaw reported to his government that there was no apparent opposition there. The new constitution acquired then, and retained afterwards, a significance far beyond what was appropriate or realistic. Edmund Burke spoke of 'this great good', and the Prussian minister, Herzberg, declared that

1 the Poles have given the *coup de grâce* to the Prussian monarchy
  by voting a constitution much better than the English. I think
  that Poland will, sooner or later, regain West Prussia, and perhaps also East Prussia. How can we defend our state . . . against
5 a numerous and well-governed nation?

Karl Marx, writing in the mid-nineteenth century, referred to what was

1 with all its faults . . . the only act of freedom which eastern

Europe had undertaken in the the midst of Prussian, Russian and Austrian barbarism. It was, moreover, initiated exclusively by the privileged classes, the nobility. The history of the world
5 knows no other example of similar noble conduct by the nobility.

Historians have written at length of the 1791 Constitution and the wonder of it. But although the commissions and other bodies which it set up began work immediately on a wide-ranging programme of social and economic reform under the slogan 'The King with the People, the People with the King', neither this social and economic package, nor the constitutional reforms of 3 May were ever put into effect. The reputation of the 1791 Constitution owes more to what was intended to happen than to what actually occurred; more to aspiration than to realisation. Its significance lies in its image, not in its reality, but it is none the less important for that. It was the Polish Bill of Rights, the embodiment of Polish expectation of freedom. Its powerful symbolism survived the death of the Republic in 1795 and the vicissitudes of the nineteenth century, so that in 1918, when the Polish Republic was restored, 3 May was chosen as the national day.

In addition to Kollataj, there were in Poland in 1791 a considerable number of politically conscious writers who had travelled widely, and many of whom had studied in France or Italy. They were well versed in developments in western Europe, particularly in France, and strongly motivated by the ideals of Liberty, Equality and Fraternity. They were in touch with the King, and regular attenders at his 'philosophical lunches' which were held on Thursdays at the Palace. Many were members of the Great *Sejm*. When news of the new constitution reached Russia, the mild reforms of Warsaw were equated to the worst excesses of the French Revolution – those involved were described as Jacobins all, and part of an international revolutionary conspiracy aimed at the overthrow of absolute monarchies everywhere. Stanislas-Augustus believed otherwise:

1 I find it unbelievable that . . . people in foreign countries can compare our revolution with the French one, seeing the great differences and contradictions existing between the two.

Catherine, however, saw, or said she saw, little to choose between revolutionary France and revolutionary Poland; something would have to be done in due course to curb such subversive activity so close to Russia.
  * In the meantime official Russian policy was to spectate, waiting quietly on the sidelines, until those Poles who had remained uncorrupted should 'invite Russia to help restore their liberties'. Catherine, writing at the end of May to the headstrong Potemkin who

was campaigning in the south against the Ottomans, warned against precipitate action in Poland. When peace had been made with the Ottomans, then Russia would be free to move against 'the new enemies' (i.e. Poland). Meanwhile, as long as the Poles made no hostile move and as long as Prussia sent no troops into Poland, Russia would wait. If, however, either of these things happened, Potemkin was to invade Poland at once in order to 'liberate people of our race and religion' from the rule of their 'unreliable king'. Two months later Catherine wrote again to Potemkin about Poland. She gave her view that the new constitution in Poland could do no good to Poland's neighbours, but that in order to act Russia needed a free hand. Peace with the Ottoman Empire was now essential. Russia could then restore the old constitution in Poland, and with it Russian security. Meanwhile, Potemkin was ordered to open negotiations with a conservative-minded group of Polish magnates who might favour forming a confederation to overthrow the new constitution.

A series of Russian victories against the Ottomans, which had begun at the end of 1790, continued into 1791 and led the Sultan to sue for peace. In August an armistice was arranged, followed by a peace treaty signed at Jassy in January 1792 (see page 141). In March Russian troops began to withdraw from the southern front. Catherine was ready to deal with Poland.

2 The War of the Second Partition 1792–3

At the end of 1791 Catherine had written that she would never agree to the new Polish constitution, proclaimed without consultation, and in alleged breach of the Russo-Polish treaties of 1768 and 1773 – especially as the whole had been carried through by the Poles 'to the accompaniment of many insults' to herself. She went on:

1 We can do whatever we want in Poland, for Vienna and Berlin will only oppose us with a pile of written paper, and we will finish our affair ourselves . . . We will always find a party [in Poland] when we need it. There are bound to be people who
5 prefer the old regime. There are many pretexts – we only need to choose.

a) The Confederation of Targowica 1792

Although Potemkin had died in August 1791, Russian negotiations had continued with the group of malcontent Polish magnates. An Act of Confederation based on Potemkin's draft was drawn up by them in St Petersburg in April 1792. To disguise its Russian sponsorship it was dated as if made a fortnight later, and at Targowica, just inside Poland. On 14 May the Polish conspirators arrived in Targowica and proclaimed the Confederation. Four days later they were joined by 97,000 Russian troops. The Confederates accused 'usurpers' of spreading a 'contagion of democratic ideas' and abolishing the 'golden freedoms' of liberty and equality (of the nobility). They called for Russian aid to restore the old constitution, in accordance with the 1773 treaty, and demanded the overthrow of the *Sejm* and a renewal of the Russian guarantee of Polish territorial integrity.

The largely untried Polish army of still no more than 37,000 could be no match for the invaders. A desperate appeal to Frederick William to honour his obligations under the treaty of 1790 fell on deaf ears. Although Frederick William had written enthusiastically to Stanislas-Augustus in May 1791, pledging his 'eagerness . . . to contribute to the support of the liberty and independence of Poland', this was at a time when the Russo-Ottoman war was still in progress and it was in Prussia's interest to support Russia's adversaries, including the Polish reformers. Frederick William justified his *volte face* in June 1792 on the grounds that 'the state of things has entirely changed since the alliance which I contracted with the Republic', and added that he did 'not consider [himself] bound by the treaty of 1790 to defend by [his] army the *hereditary* monarchy as established by the Constitution of 3 May 1791'.

b) Prussia, Austria and France

In February 1792 Prussia and Austria had signed an anti-revolutionary alliance against France, pledging support for the principles of absolute monarchy wherever they might be threatened. Among the other clauses of the alliance was one binding the two countries to maintain the territorial integrity of Poland and to support its new constitution. The original negotiations at the end of 1791 had referred to *the* new Polish constitution. But Leopold of Austria, although not unsympathetic to the 3 May Constitution, knew that without Prussian help he could not hope to save his Belgian provinces, or save Louis XVI and his Austrian Queen. He, therefore, bowed to Prussian pressure and agreed to an emendation of the final text to read *a* new constitution. From that moment the Prusso-Polish treaty was a dead letter. Prussia was already looking towards a further partition of Poland as compensation for supporting Austria in a war against France.

In March Leopold of Austria died, to be succeeded by his son, Francis, a much more warlike monarch than his father. Within two months, Austria was at war with France. This necessarily involved Prussia under the terms of the Austro-Prussian alliance, and the two countries prepared to invade France with the object of putting down the revolution. This was good news for Catherine. When the end of the Ottoman war in January 1792 had left her free to send troops into

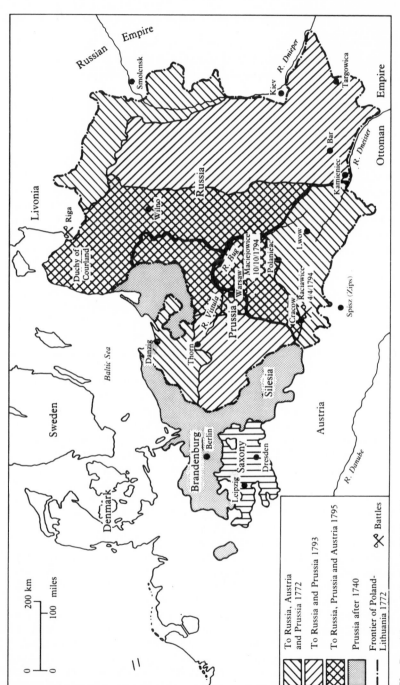

The Partitions of Poland 1772–95

Poland, all that had been necessary was to ensure that she was able to do so unhindered by Prussia or Austria. Without effort on her part, Prussia and Austria had played into her hands. Catherine encouraged them further. In a spirit of apparent self-sacrifice, she relinquished her right under the Austro-Russian treaty of 1781 to call on Austria for help against rebel factions in Poland. Austria could not be expected to fight revolution both in France and in Poland – Russia would therefore take on the latter task singlehanded. As far as Prussia was concerned, negotiations through the Prussian ambassador in St Petersburg made it clear to Frederick William that Catherine *would* be prepared to associate Prussia in a future partition of Poland, provided that Prussia took an active part, with Austria, in the war against France. This would prevent any possible Austrian intervention in Poland while Russia was restoring the old constitution there. Prussian intervention in turn was prevented when, on 7 August 1792, Frederick William signed a convention agreeing not to interfere with Russia's activities in Poland, providing that he should eventually receive a share of the spoils.

To maintain appearances Prussia associated herself with Austria in issuing a cordial invitation to Catherine to join them in the French enterprise. Catherine politely declined. She wrote to Francis:

1 It is well indeed for a young sovereign to commence his career with an enterprise, which has for its object the preservation of Europe from the contagion of an example so scandalous and baneful. But that which has happened in a country so far removed
5 as France is from my own State, has called my attention to what is occurring in my own neighbourhood. The subversion of the Constitution of Poland by the new Constitution of 3 May, 1791, will produce disorders analagous to those of France.

Elsewhere at this time she wrote of 'the Jacobins of Warsaw who are in close correspondence with those of Paris', and of her pressing need to deal with them. 'I will fight the enemy in Poland, and in so doing I shall not the less occupy myself with the affairs of France.'

The invasion of France by Prussia and Austria was unsuccessful. In September the Prussians were defeated at Valmy with heavy losses. As a result, Frederick William announced that he would not continue the war unless he had an absolute assurance of an indemnity in the form of Polish territory, to compensate him for his expenses. Prussian help remained essential to Austria and Francis was therefore forced to agree to Frederick William's demands. Austria still hoped to obtain compensation from France. This hope received a near fatal blow when in November the Austrian army was severely defeated at Jemappes. This left most of the Austrian Netherlands in French hands, and put an end to a long-cherished imperial plan to arrange an exchange of the

Austrian Netherlands for Bavaria. Francis had hoped to make such an exchange part of his 'compensation' for the war against France.

c) Events in Poland 1792

While Prussia and Austria were occupied with preparations for their French expedition, Russian troops spread across Poland in support of the Confederation of Targowica. The Confederates quickly formed an executive committee, the Generality, and established it as a Russian puppet government. On 22 May Stanislas-Augustus was made 'dictator' of Poland by the desperate *Sejm*. This was of little avail. The Russians entered Wilno, and a Russian-sponsored Confederation of Lithuania, similar to the Confederation of Targowica, set itself up in the Grand Duchy as the legitimate government based on the old constitution. Stanislas-Augustus entered into direct negotiations with Catherine for a four-week truce. His overtures were rejected. He then wrote her a personal letter, referring to the intimate relations they had once enjoyed, and asking for an eternal alliance and an advantageous commercial treaty between the two countries. As a means of guaranteeing this and 'providing for a stronger and better government for Poland', he even offered the reversion of the Polish crown to Catherine's younger grandson, Constantine. (This was a measure of his desperation, for the May Constitution, by which he was bound, had made the crown hereditary in the Wettin family.) Catherine rejected the offer. Stanislas-Augustus appealed round Europe for help. Austria 'saw no reason to oppose the wishes of Catherine'; France considered the Polish revolution insufficiently democratic to be worth supporting; England and Holland refused assistance on the grounds that 'no intervention on their part could be serviceable to Poland, without much greater exertion and expense than the maintenance of their separate interests could possibly justify'. Clearly, no help was available anywhere. It was not only Prussia which had abandoned Poland.

Stanislas-Augustus had no choice but to agree to the demands of the Confederates. Suddenly, in July, he announced a ceasefire and his acceptance of the Confederation of Targowica as the rightful government of Poland. Why did he do it? Was he the weak and cowardly traitor many thought him? It seems most probable that he acted from the best of motives. His army was heavily outnumbered (almost 3 to 1), he had no allies on whom he could call, his country had been overrun by foreign troops and, worst of all, his people were divided and once again in a state of civil war. In addition, he was himself no soldier, nor leader of men. The best he could do was to save further bloodshed.

* Towards the end of 1792 Catherine began to think seriously about a second partition of Poland. While her motives are not entirely clear, it appears that she had earlier in the year intended simply to

restore the unreformed Polish constitution and re-establish Poland as a Russian protectorate. She had to weigh up the long-term advantages of governing indirectly the whole of what remained of Poland, against the short-term gains to be obtained by annexation of a smaller area of rich land, peopled by those of 'Russian faith and race'. A number of events made up her mind in favour of partition. The difficulties of reasserting Russian control over Poland were much greater than expected, for the Confederates had proved incompetent in government. There was also a need to make good the promise given to Prussia of land in Poland, in order to keep her in the war against France. But a unilateral aggrandisement of Prussia would upset the balance of power: the only solution was a bilateral partition, Russia's share of which would be 'compensation' for the expenses and loss of men incurred in restoring right government to Poland. Then, just before Christmas 1792, the Emperor Francis made direct contact with Catherine. He claimed for Austria a share in Poland equal to that which might be taken by Prussia or Russia, now that the fortunes of war had destroyed his hope of effecting the Netherlands exchange. Catherine ignored his claim, but it must have been clear to her that she could not continue to do so indefinitely. If partition by Russia and Prussia was to be accomplished without difficulty, it must be entered into immediately. In January 1793 she gave Frederick William the go-ahead to invade Poland. He happily did so, having first issued a suitable manifesto referring to the need to suppress 'the principles of Jacobinism and the spirit of French democracy' which were taking root in Poland. The Russian troops were, of course, already there.

3 The Second Partition 1793

In January 1793 a second Treaty of Partition between Russia and Prussia was drawn up. It was justified on the grounds of the political dangers to neighbouring states which would arise from the spread of French revolutionary ideas in Poland. Russia was to have the Ukraine, Podolia and the eastern half of Lithuania, totalling 250,200 square kilometres and three million people, while Prussia's share was to include the whole of Wielkopolska (Great Poland), together with the German-speaking areas of Danzig and Thorn, and about one million people. Austria was to be fobbed off with assurances that Prussia would continue to fight alongside her in the war against France, and that both Prussia and Russia would support her in furthering the Netherlands-Bavarian exchange, should it ever prove possible to carry out.

In April manifestos were issued announcing the proposed partition. The news was received with consternation by the Confederates of Targowica. This was not at all what they had intended, and they did not accept Catherine's claim that Russia was entitled to a slice of Poland as compensation for expenses involved in coming to their aid.

Even less did they accept the need to provide Prussia with compensation for the war against France. Catherine wrote, in typical fashion, to Count Sievers, her ambassador in Warsaw:

1 From the beginning we have attempted to found our relations with Poland on an enduring basis, but the Poles, instead of meeting our advances with corresponding friendship, have only manifested the bitterest hatred . . .

She continued with complaints that the Confederates had proved to be untrustworthy and selfish and that Stanislas-Augustus was stirring up his people against Russia, and concluded:

1 By adopting this plan [of partition] we agree to an act whose whole result is to liberate from oppression all Russian lands and cities peopled, or founded, by a cognate race, and confessing the same faith as ourselves.

As in 1773, it was important to preserve appearances. Everything needed to be done legally and decently. Stanislas-Augustus was persuaded, by the Russian offer of a future gift of 34 million Polish florins needed to pay his debts, to summon what proved to be the last *Sejm* of the Republic's history. A carefully selected and suitably rewarded body of deputies met at Grodno. Surrounded by Russian soldiers, the *Sejm* was first forced to reverse all the legislation of the previous five years. The 1791 Constitution was rescinded and the old constitution with its 'Golden Freedoms' was reinstated. Then the treaties of partition between Poland and Russia and Poland and Prussia were presented for approval. Threats of sequestration of their lands and of deportation to Siberia left the deputies with little choice but to assent to all the measures put before them. The best they could manage was a silent protest on the occasion of the ratification of the treaty with Prussia. On the principle that 'silence means consent', the Russians declared the treaty approved. The King, mindful of his financial situation, signed the necessary documents. The partition treaty with Russia became effective in July 1793 and that with Prussia in September (see map on page 96).

Before the *Sejm* dispersed in October 1793 it was called upon to ratify a further treaty, a defensive alliance between Russia and what remained of the Polish state. This returned Poland to her former status as a Russian protectorate. The old, unreformed constitution was again guaranteed by Russia, and was not to be changed in any way without Russian consent. Poland was to make no alliances other than with Russia, and Russian troops were to be allowed into Poland, although only after consultation with the Polish government. The inclusion of this proviso angered Catherine when she heard about it. She wrote:

 1 My intention had been to divert the attention of other governments from the entrance of any troops into Poland, so as imper-
   ceptibly to accustom them to this in all cases. The Polish government would have been spared inevitable explanations; if it
 5 was asked on what terms the troops entered, it would have merely
   needed to reply in accordance with the treaty and no more. It is
   obvious I would not take on the burden of defending a weak
   state unless I could count on complete submission to my advice,
   plans and views. Whom now shall I have to ask to agree to the
10 action of my forces? The king? But he has no power. The *Sejm*?
   But then I would have to explain my reasons every time . . .

On hearing the terms of the treaty a Polish deputy exclaimed,

 1 Poland has become a Russian province. We would have done
   better to unite entirely with Russia before; we would have maintained more of our integrity and we would have been happier!

The Russian ambassador advised Catherine of the need to keep a tight control over Stanislas-Augustus:

 1 We must hold the rod over him . . . his task must be assigned to
   him . . . he will receive a master, under the title of Russian
   ambassador . . .

The ambassador was instructed by Catherine to form a party independent of the king through which to work, and to fill government posts with 'faithful and modest people'.
   * The Second Partition, which she had engineered, was a political triumph for Catherine, but what one historian has called her 'hypocrisy and flagrant breach of promises' were criticised by a Russian statesman of the time:

 1 The thing itself is too notoriously unjust, but the perfidious
   manner in which it was executed, renders it still more shocking.
   Since we were determined to commit this injustice, we ought to
   have said frankly that we were robbing Poland to avenge our-
 5 selves because she had tried to make an offensive alliance against
   us; but instead we talked of friendship, we published manifestos
   to say that we were seeking only the happiness of Poland, that
   we wished to assure to her the integrity of her possessions and
   the enjoyment of her old government . . .

Although his share of territory was less than Catherine's, Frederick William benefited substantially by the acquisition, at last, of Danzig. He benefited also by the exclusion of Austria from the partition. It was a serious diplomatic defeat for Austria, tipping the balance of power against her not only in Germany, but also in eastern Europe generally. The inexperience of the young Emperor and his continued pursuit of the Bavarian exchange plan when it had clearly become unworkable, contributed to Austria's exclusion from the Polish share-out. Poland was left further disabled – less than half her territory now remained, with only about four million inhabitants – all under tighter Russian control than ever.

Although historians, with hindsight, have seen the Second Partition as decisive, it was not at the time inevitable that there should be a third and final partition only two years later. At the end of 1793, Prussia, the greediest of the three powers (perhaps because she was also the smallest), was already favouring another, and total, partition. But then Prussia had always been the strongest supporter and proponent of partition. Austria, although smarting from the humiliations of the Second Partition, was in fact opposed to any further partitions, at least for the foreseeable future. Catholic Austria had never been as wholeheartedly in favour of dismembering Catholic Poland as the other two powers. Russia appeared at first undecided, although under the influence of Count Sievers Catherine soon came to be of the opinion that a further partition would be necessary eventually. There was, she believed, no great urgency, for Russia held Poland in a firm grip. The events of the next few months altered her opinion.

4 The National Rising 1793–4

The winter of 1793–4 brought unrest in Poland. Government ministers and officials abandoned their posts, and the administration ground to a halt. Most of the wealthy patriots went into voluntary exile – some to Saxony, others to Austria or France. The army was reduced to less than 15,000 men, leaving twice as many able-bodied fighting men without means of support to become vagrants. The majority drifted to Warsaw where they joined the existing urban poor, and formed a disaffected 'rabble', simply waiting for a leader to rouse them to action. The Polish economy began to collapse – six banks in Warsaw failed in 1793 – as the country struggled to support a large occupying army of around 40,000 men. *Coups* were planned and conspiracies were formed everywhere. Revolution was in the air, encouraged by news from France. The Russians applied a heavy hand to suppress local outbreaks, arresting anyone suspected of subversive activity, and in February 1794 ordered a further reduction in the Polish army. Only an uprising of the whole Polish nation, a *levée-en-masse*, could match the resources of the enemy.

* The uprising came with the return of Tadeusz Kosciuszko. He was an idealist, a patriot and a revolutionary, with great personal courage and qualities of leadership. After being educated at Poland's military academy, he completed five years' military training in France. When he returned to Poland he found he could not afford to buy a commission, and went instead with a group of French volunteers to North America where he fought in the American War of Independence as an officer-engineer and one of Washington's aides. When that war ended he returned to Poland to live quietly in the country, farming his land, until 1789 when he was asked to help reform and modernise the Polish army, whose second-in-command he became. After the Second Partition he went into exile in Saxony. He returned to Poland a year later.

On 24 March 1794 Kosciuszko read out the *Act of Insurrection of the Citizens and Inhabitants of the Palatinate of Cracow* at a pre-arranged rendezvous in the market square of Cracow. A splendid figure in national costume and with a feather in his hat, he took an oath:

1 I Tadeusz Kosciuszko swear before God and to the whole Polish nation, that I shall employ the authority vested in me for the integrity of the frontiers, for gaining national self-rule and for the foundation of general liberty, and not for private benefit. So
5 help me, Lord God.

On a wave of patriotic emotion the crowd of citizens followed his example and swore to 'free the country from shameful oppression and the foreign yoke, or to perish and be buried in the ruins'.

A Supreme National Council was appointed to take over government, and all men aged between 18 and 28 were to be conscripted, noble and non-noble alike, in all areas to which the insurrection spread. On 4 April Kosciuszko, with 4000 soldiers and 2000 peasants armed with scythes, defeated the Russians at Raclawice. The battle was decided by the heroic charge of the scythemen, who captured the Russian guns. The very last ceremonial ennoblement in the Republic's history took place after the battle. It was that of a peasant, who had been first to reach the guns and had put his cap over the muzzle of a cannon, much to the astonishment of the Russian gunner.

A fortnight later the people of Warsaw rose in revolt, led by a cobbler (or, according to some sources, a tailor), accompanied, appropriately, by members of the Guild of Slaughterers. The following day, Good Friday, turned into an orgy of killing. Russian troops were driven through the streets and 4000 of them died there. The Russian ambassador prudently fled. In the next few days, leading members of the Confederation of Targowica were rounded up, tried and hanged. A number of other people suspected of being spies were lynched by the mob. Much the same scenes occurred in Wilno, the Lithuanian capital, where an 'Act of

The Scythemen

Insurrection of the Lithuanian Nation' was proclaimed. The King, who had remained inactive and alone in Warsaw Castle, sanctioned the setting up of an Insurrectionary Government.

* On 7 May Kosciuszko issued the Manifesto of Polaniec which gave the peasants personal freedom and reduced their labour dues. (This Manifesto was never implemented, but its very existence gave substance to the Russian belief that the Insurrection was Jacobin in character.) The Insurrectionary Government quickly found itself in some difficulties. There was a lack of certainty about the political character of the insurrection itself – some extreme Jacobins were certainly involved, but so also were some conservative magnates. The King donated all his table-silver to help finance government expenditure, but most of the *szlachta* remained on the side-lines. There were additional problems of widespread chaos and food shortages, but despite these the Insurrectionary Government achieved results. Kollataj, put in charge of the Treasury, introduced a graded tax scheme, issued a new currency, and confiscated some church property. Armament factories were taken over, but, although enough cannon could be produced there was a severe shortage of small arms. As a result, in any engagement the rebel army had to rely heavily on the cavalry, supported by artillery and massed peasant scythemen.

By June 1794 Catherine decided that the time had come 'to extinguish the last spark of fire in Poland'. As Austria's Netherlands campaign had failed, Francis turned his eyes to Poland. Catherine did not discourage these overtures for a share in any further partition, for Austria would serve as a useful counterbalance to Prussian demands. Frederick William, aware of Austria's moves, immediately offered Catherine military assistance in the expectation of rewards for himself. Prussian troops were despatched towards Cracow, and occupied the city after defeating the insurgents. Kosciuszko retreated to the safety of Warsaw with what remained of his army. A few weeks later Wilno fell to the Russians.

In mid-July a combined Russo-Prussian army of 40,000 laid siege to the poorly defended city of Warsaw. Nevertheless, little progress had been made by the attackers, when in September news came of a serious revolt in Prussian-occupied Wielkopolska. Frederick William was forced to withdraw his men from outside Warsaw, in order to deal with it. Catherine is reported 'to have laughed heartily' at his discomfiture, for it could only strengthen her hand if Russian troops took Warsaw unaided. Catherine ordered General Suvarov to move towards Warsaw with reinforcements from the south. In early October Kosciuszko marched out of the city with 7,000 ill-trained men in an attempt to cut off these Russian reinforcements numbering twice as many well-seasoned troops. Kosciusko was heavily defeated at Maciejowice. He is said to have had three horses killed under him in the battle before, badly wounded, he was taken prisoner together with several of his generals. At the moment of his fall from the third horse, Kosciuszko was alleged to have cried 'Finis Poloniae' ('This is the end of Poland'). He did not, in fact, do so, although he would certainly have subscribed to the sentiments. His loss was a serious blow to the Insurrectionary Government whose army was now leaderless. The end of Poland was very near.

   * Suvarov announced his intention of storming Praga, a fortified

Tadeusz Kosciuszko

suburb of Warsaw and separated from it only by the River Vistula. At the beginning of November the Russians destroyed Praga in a surpise dawn attack. 20,000 Poles were killed, many more drowned in the Vistula and 10,000 were taken prisoner. Russian losses were minimal. The streets, strewn with dead bodies, literally ran with blood. Russian soldiers massacred the citizens – 'they are dogs, let them perish'. Women, children, priests and nuns had their skulls split with hatchets, according to Russian eyewitnesses. The British ambassador, William Gardner, sent back a vivid and heartrending account of what he saw and heard:

1 the most horrid and unnecessary barbarities, houses burnt, women massacred, infants at the breast pierced with the pikes of Cosaques [Cossacks], and universal plunder . . .

It was a terrible revenge for the 4000 Russians who had died in the Warsaw streets two years earlier. Suvarov was reported to be deeply moved by the scenes going on around him. If so, he did little to stop them, for not until late in the day did he make any attempt to restrain his men. It appears most probable that he had lost control of them, and was forced to allow them a period of licence. Nevertheless, he was apparantly happy enough with his victory to send a joking report to Catherine, 'Hurrah – Praga – Suvarov', to which she is said to have replied, equally briefly, 'Bravo – Fieldmarshal – Catherine'.

On 8 November Warsaw surrendered. Suvarov marched into the city, amidst cries of 'Long live Catherine!' Stanislas-Augustus remained in the city as king until it was declared conquered territory at the end of the month. Then he was put into a coach and sent to Grodno, where he was forced to abdicate. His debts were paid as promised, and he was provided with a pension. Escorted by Russian dragoons he was driven away into exile. One of those who saw him go was William Gardner, who had known the King personally. 'It is impossible for any person really attached to royalty, not to feel most sensibly on such an occasion', he wrote sadly. Stanislas-Augustus spent the rest of his life – he died in 1798 – in St Petersburg, where he occupied his time planning the recovery of his throne. He was given a state funeral by Catherine's son and successor, Paul I, who a year earlier had celebrated his mother's death by freeing Kosciuszko and other Polish prisoners of war.

5 The Third Partition 1795

With the fall of Warsaw and the exile of the King the Republic was *in extremis*. Catherine proclaimed her belief that Kosciuszko was a spokesman for 'undiluted Jacobinism, full of French principles of absurd equality and transient freedoms'. She found like minds among her ministers, who declared:

1 The state of mind of the Poles, particularly young ones, is such that the infection could easily spread; the freedom of peasants and such like would provoke our village dwellers, so similar in language and habits.

She had made up her mind. The revolutionary spirit must be crushed, once and for all, in Poland. There could be no alternative to the total annihilation of Poland in a final partition.

The negotiations between the partitioning powers were to be long-drawn out. With Poland 'dead and gone for ever, and not to be called to life again', this third and final partition would bring the frontiers of the three powers into contact for the first time. Prussia and Austria were already on bad terms, as a result of the débâcle of the invasion of France and the exclusion of Austria from the Second Partition. The choice of defensible frontier lines in Poland was therefore of supreme importance to all three. Russia and Austria quickly agreed on their shares and on the need to restrict further territorial gains by Prussia. Frederick William proved difficult. He insisted that unless Prussia retained Cracow (already occupied by his troops, but long coveted by Austria) he would not proceed. Without his cooperation, he asserted, this final partition would be impossible. Catherine called his bluff. She decided to proceed, at least for the time being, with Austria alone. A secret treaty between the two powers was drawn up and signed in January 1795. The preamble read:

1 Poland having been entirely subjected and conquered by the arms of the Empress of Russia, she has determined to arrange with her allies for a complete partition of that state, which has shown an absolute incapacity to form a government which will
5 enable it to live peaceably under the laws, or to maintain itself in independence.

By the terms of this partition agreement Russia would acquire 180,000 square miles of Lithuania, the remainder of Belorussia, the western Ukraine and overlordship of Courland, with a total population of about six million. Austria would receive 45,000 square miles with about three million inhabitants. The remaining area, 57,000 square miles containing about two and a half million people was allocated to Prussia (see map on page 96). The Russian share was equal to that of Austria and Prussia put together, but then as the Russian representative said:

1 . . . the title of the Empress to her portion of Poland is not the

work of a moment or of chance, but the creation of thirty years
of labour, cares and colossal efforts of every kind . . . in comparison with these, Austria and Prussia have received as an
5 unbought gift all the advantages which they have reaped and will
reap in Poland.

When six months later he had still not agreed to the partition,
Frederick William was given an ultimatum to surrender Cracow or
face military action. Seriously afraid of war against the combined
forces of Russia and Austria, he gave way and withdrew from Cracow,
leaving it for Austria. Catherine at the same time withdrew from
Warsaw in favour of Prussia. In October 1795 Austro-Prussian and
Prusso-Russian treaties were signed. The Third Partition had been
made. This time there was no Polish king or government to consult,
nor any *Sejm* to ratify the treaties.

Sorting out the details took the three powers nearly two years to
complete. The final Treaty of Partition was signed in St Petersburg by
Russia, Prussia and Austria in January 1797. A secret and separate
article read:

1 In view of the necessity to abolish everything which could revive
the memory of the existence of the Kingdom of Poland, now
that the annulment of this body politic has been effected . . . the
high contracting parties are agreed and undertake never to
5 include in their titles . . . the name or designation of the Kingdom of Poland, which shall remain suppressed as from the present and forever . . .

The Polish body politic appeared to be well and truly buried.

6 Aftermath

The dying gasps of the Polish Republic excited little interest elsewhere
in Europe. It was France and the events there upon which attention
was focused. Most of the diplomats stationed in Warsaw had left by
1794. Early in 1795 the remaining ambassadors were informed that
their missions were at an end, for with the exile of the King, 'the
court to which you are accredited has ceased to exist'. By the time the
final Treaty of Partition was signed in January 1797 only William
Gardner was left, and that was only because he could not afford to go.
He had been feeding 300 refugees in the British embassy, and was
bankrupt. Pleas to London for payment of his salary were ignored.
Not until December 1797 did he receive £2000 enabling him to pay off
his creditors and leave Poland. With his departure the old order in

Warsaw finally came to an end. It was *Finis Poloniae* – but, despite the secret article of the Third Partition, *not* forever.

Making notes on *'The Partitions of Poland: The Second and Third Partitions 1793 and 1795'*

This chapter outlines the momentous events in Poland between the years 1788 and 1795 which ended with the destruction of Poland. A great deal happened in a short time and you need to be clear about the sequence of events. 'Reasons and responsibility' for the Partitions will be discussed fully in the next chapter but, from information in this and earlier chapters, you have probably formed your own views on

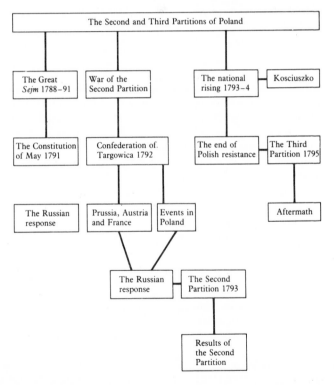

Summary – The Partitions of Poland: The Second and Third Partitions 1793 and 1795

why the Partitions happened and *who* was responsible. These are not easy questions, for there are no simple answers.

Making notes using the chapter headings and sub-headings may help to clarify your ideas.

Source-based questions on 'The Partitions of Poland: The Second and Third Partitions 1793 and 1795'

1 The 1791 Constitution
Read the series of short extracts on pages 91–7. Answer the following questions:

a) Explain 'the ancient faults of our system of government' (page 91, line 2). (2 marks)

b) What assumption does the preamble to the 1791 Constitution (page 91) make about a national constitution? (1 mark)

c) What is Karl Marx's attitude to the Constitution (page 92–3)? Why might it be considered surprising? Explain your answer. (3 marks)

d) In her letter to the Emperor Francis what does Catherine declare to be her objection to the 1791 Constitution (page 97)? How far is this consistent with her argument on page 94? (6 marks)

e) Compare Catherine's views with those of the Prussian minister (page 92) and of Stanislas-Augustus (page 93). What conclusions can be drawn regarding the sincerity of the authors? (8 marks)

2 The Second Partition
Read the series of short extracts on pages 100–1. Answer the following questions:

a) What in the first two extracts does Catherine declare is the justification for her part in the Second Partition? What are the points of criticism made by the Russian statesman (page 101)? How valid are these criticisms? Explain your answer. (7 marks)

b) The Polish deputy in the second sentence of his remarks quoted on page 101 makes a large assumption. What is it? What evidence is there to substantiate it? (4 marks)

c) Explain Catherine's anger in the extract on page 101. (3 marks)

d) What types of evidence are (i) most reliable, and (ii) least reliable when reaching conclusions about the motives of the participants in the Partitions of Poland? Explain your answer. (6 marks)

3 The Third Partition

Read the extracts on pages 108 and 109. Answer the following questions:

a) The preamble to the Russo-Austrian Treaty (page 108) contains a number of sweeping statements. Examine them critically and write a few sentences correcting those which are erroneous. (6 marks)

b) What are likely to have been the Russian motives for making these statements? (3 marks)

c) What is the Russian representative's argument in support of Catherine's very extensive acqusitions in Poland (page 108–09)? Would her allies have been convinced by it? Explain your answer. (5 marks)

d) Explain 'the body politic' (line 3) and 'the high contracting parties' (line 4) in the secret article (page 109). What was 'the necessity' referred to in line 1? How was it effected? (5 marks)

e) Why were the Partitions of Poland all given a legal form? What does this suggest about the way in which foreign relations were conducted during the period? (6 marks)

4 Illustrations

Carefully study the illustrations of Augustus the Strong (front cover), 'Catherine's entry into St Petersburg' (page 37), Stanislas-Augustus (page 71), 'The Royal Cake' (page 77), Kosciuszko (page 106), and 'the Scythemen' (page 104). Answer the following questions:

a) The portraits of Augustus and Stanislas-Augustus were both painted so as to please the person portrayed. The techniques used by the two artists to do this were similar. What were these techniques? What can be learnt about the attitudes and values of the time from these portraits? (6 marks)

b) Stanislas-Augustus is portrayed very differently in his portrait and in 'The Royal Cake'. Explain these differences. (4 marks)

c) How far can 'Catherine's entry into St Petersburg' and 'the Scythemen' be relied upon as accurate representations of what happened on each occasion? Explain your answer. (5 marks)

d) The artist who drew the portrait of Kosciuszko was attempting to endow his subject with a particular 'image'. What was this image, and how did the artist attempt to create it? (4 marks)

e) Discuss the opinion that 'illustrations from the pre-photographic age are of no significant use to historians'. (6 marks)

CHAPTER 8

The Partitions of Poland: Reasons, Responsibilities and Results

For the last two centuries historians have been writing at length on the partitions of Poland – not just on the events, but also on their causes and effects. The views expressed have been diverse as the topic is one which arouses strong and often fiercely partisan emotions. It is not surprising, therefore, that some of what has been written is intemperate, biased or ill-founded. Sometimes it is all three.

1 Historical Views

Why do the partitions evoke such passion? Why was 'the death of old Poland . . . one of the most poignant moments in European history'? Were these seizures of Polish territory at the end of the eighteenth century worse than all the many other seizures of other territory in other countries before and after that date? Throughout history states have been swallowed up by greedy neighbours – Poland herself did not have an unblemished record as an acquirer of other states' land. Yet, if Poland's fate was not in itself exceptional, why did it create such a profound impression? Historians have struggled with this problem but have produced no one satisfactory answer. However, it seems probable that the timing of the events was significant. A new spirit of nationalism, combined with the ideals of liberty and equality, was appearing on the European scene and was in stark contrast to the political chicanery of the partitions, called by a speaker in the House of Commons 'the most flagrant instance of profligate perfidy which has ever disgraced the annals of mankind'. It was this contrast which made the partitions seem even worse than they were, and led members of the romantic movement to embrace the Polish cause at the beginning of the nineteenth century. They built up the whole sorry business of the partitions into a monumental tragedy, which had destroyed a Poland peopled by colourful, if disorganised, swash-buckling nobles and happy, hardworking peasants. This romanticised and idyllic view of Poland had the opposite result to that intended. Instead of arousing sympathy for the old Poland it provided, in the Polish people and their institutions, ideal scapegoats for the apologists of the partitioning powers: the Poles had brought their troubles on themselves.

The three partitioning powers, especially Prussia, and later Germany in general, spent much of the nineteenth century trying to justify their actions to the world by denigrating the Poles as inferiors, a worthless people, charming but incompetent, who had none of the Protestant virtues of thrift and hardwork.

1 The Poles have never done anything in history, except commit outrageous quarrelsome stupidities. It would be impossible to cite a single occasion when Poland had successfully represented progress or done anything whatsoever of historical significance.

This was manifestly untrue, and was written in 1851 by Friedrich Engels – a German who should have known better. Similar sentiments have been expressed by historians, some of whom have gone further:

1 As the Slav has never shown any capacity for civilisation, the proper method is . . . to colonise his territory with sturdy Teutons, to leave him, if at all, only in a completely inferior position with no separate political existence.

This was written c. 1900, not by a German, but by a British historian, C. Fletcher. Until the 1914–18 war most British historians (with a few exceptions, notably Macaulay), accepted the German point of view on the Poles and their shortcomings. Fletcher sees the whole issue in racial terms, something which, unfortunately, is not exceptional in nineteenth-century historical writing on Poland.

The First World War changed the opinion of British historians quite radically. Lord Eversley's standard work on the partitions, published in 1915, is very much a product of its time. While admonishing Russia and Austria for their part in the destruction of Poland, his severest censure is reserved for Prussia. For neither Frederick II nor Frederick William has he a good word to say. In any discussion of the partitions most British historians since Eversley's time have tended to place at least as much emphasis on the wrongdoing of the partitioning powers as on the failings of the Poles.

In 1869, a Polish deputy in the German Parliament quoted Macaulay on 'the crime of the partitions'. In his reply Bismarck, the German Chancellor, sought to justify the dismemberment of the Polish Republic. In doing so he brought together many of the arguments which have been used by historians as well as by politicians:

1 The Polish Republic owed its destruction much less to foreigners than to the inconceivable worthlessness of those persons who represented the Polish nation when it was broken up . . . The participation of the Germans in the mutilation of Poland was a
5 necessary compliance with the law of self-preservation . . . If you contest the right of conquest, you cannot have read the history of your own country. It is thus that states are formed . . .

The Poles themselves committed the crime of conquest a hundredfold . . . instead of grumbling perpetually the Poles . . .
10 should gratefully acknowledge all that has been done for their country. Germanisation has been pursued by culture . . . [The Poles] enjoy a degree of well-being such as never existed, nor was ever dreamed of within the Polish realm since the commencement of history . . . I can assure you that Polish rule was
15 an infamously bad one, and that is why it shall never be revived . . .

Were Bismarck and other Prussian apologists right in declaring that the fault lay with the Poles themselves and that it was the internal weakness of the Polish state, 'the cowardly king and the selfish magnates' unfit to govern, which brought the Republic to an end? Or was it the case that 'the real villains were the three eastern monarchies, Poland's powerful and ambitious neighbours'? If they *were* the villains, could they, as Bismarck suggests, plead 'the law of self-preservation'?

2 Poland's Internal Weakness

Standing accused as responsible for this weakness are King Stanislas-Augustus and the *szlachta*.

a) Stanislas-Augustus

Stanislas-Augustus has been dismissed as 'the peruked nonentity', 'weak and cowardly', 'effeminate, soft and over-refined' and 'entirely led by pleasure'. 'Poor, foolish Poniatowski, an empty, windy creature, redolent of macassar', as Carlyle unkindly said of him, was not the man for the age. Therein lay his tragedy. 'If only', wrote his nephew, the commander of the Polish army in 1792, 'Your Majesty together with the *szlachta* had taken horse, had armed the townsmen and freed the peasants, Poland would now be a power – or we should have perished with honour.' Unfortunately for the King and for his country, it was not in his nature to act thus heroically. Although the son of a famous soldier, Hetman of the Korona, Stanislas-Augustus was no military leader himself. He lacked physical courage, and in moments of national disaster tended to disappear from public gaze. In 1795 he remained, almost alone, in the castle of Warsaw, and took no part in the final struggle.

Although he was vain, fond of pleasure and luxurious living, he had a strong sense of duty and a deep love of Poland. He was aware of his country's shortcomings and was genuinely concerned to promote reform of its ramshackle administration. He had been elected to the

Sejm on six separate occasions before he became king, and so had a good understanding of its workings. In 1766, soon after the signing of the Russo-Prussian agreement, he had himself written a political pamphlet, *Considerations of a Good Citizen*, exhorting the Poles to maintain their independence and their national dignity in the face of foreign violence. Later he encouraged political discussion at court, and was personally involved in drawing up the 1791 Constitution. He was not of royal blood and he felt this to be to his disadvantage. He knew that he was regarded as an upstart, who had reached the throne not by birth, nor by military prowess but through the favour of Catherine II. Many Poles thought him a Russian tool, and indeed the manner of his accession placed him in a weak position in relation both to Poland's powerful neighbours and to his own subjects.

* It was through the arts that Stanislas-Augustus left his mark on Poland for all time. Clever, cultured and cosmopolitan, he brought Poland out of what has been described as 'near medieval darkness' into the Enlightenment of the late eighteenth century, and in doing so gave his name to the last age of the Republic. His court was a centre of intellectual life. Round him were gathered Polish and foreign philosophers, writers, artists and musicians. Literature and architecture flourished under his patronage as never before in Poland. The palaces which he built to neo-classical designs were no mere copies of French or Italian models, but the beginning of a new and essentially Polish style of architecture. The magnates were encouraged to follow the royal example and all over Poland palaces and country houses sprang up, all built in the Stanislavian style. By the end of the century this style had spread throughout eastern Europe and into Russia. Education, too, benefited from the King's interest, and new schools and colleges were established with his active support. It was no longer fashionable to boast that:

1 My father and grandfather were like me, could scarcely spell out a sentence or sign their name, but they lived long, and my children will be healthy without schooling too . . .

Education through 'exposure to beauty' as a means of improving the morals of his people was a project close to Stanislas-Augustus's heart. With this end in view he established the first art gallery of any size in Poland. Opinions are divided about whether he succeeded in his aim, but at least one writer thought he had:

1 The coarse habits of our forefathers have almost vanished . . . passions common among us in other days as the result of idleness and ignorance now have no place.

Stanislas-Augustus encouraged contacts with the world outside

Poland. He invited foreign craftsmen, artists and experts of all kinds to his court, where he took many of them into his own service. The economic developments, too, of the years between the first and second partitions were largely due to his influence and patronage (see page 85). By the 1780s he was well on the way to achieving his long declared aim 'to recreate the Polish world' by opening it up to new ideas and experiences, while at the same time ensuring that the legacy of Poland's past would remain to inspire her future.

Ironically, Stanislas-Augustus's greatest achievement held the seeds of his downfall. While his exorbitant expenditure on the arts was not, in his view, mere frivolity, but part of his serious purpose for Poland, this was not the opinion of the majority of his subjects. Amongst them his massive debts did nothing to enhance his reputation. In a time of peace, and in a country where harmony reigned, Stanislas-Augustus would have made an excellent king. As it was, he was no match for the troubles which beset him, at home and abroad.

b) The *Szlachta*

The unreformed constitution of Poland was designed for the benefit of the *szlachta* in general and of the magnates in particular. It was in the interest of them all to maintain it and to retain the 'Golden Freedom' (see page 15). This severely limited the King's freedom of action. 'Free' royal elections led to factionalism and outside interference in Polish affairs. Once elected, the *Pacta Conventa* put the King in the position not of a constitutional monarch but of a manager under contract; failure to meet the terms of the contract led to the 'Right to Resist' and armed Confederation, while the *liberum veto* made the *Sejm* unworkable. The *szlachta's* insistence that political rights and financial privileges should be restricted to themselves undermined the political, social and economic stability of the state. Only a monarch of exceptional ability and strength of character and with a successful military record – like Jan Sobieski, the victor over the Ottomans outside Vienna in 1683 – could hope to impose any sort of control over what several historians refer to as 'a vicious political system'. Stanislas-Augustus was not in that mould.

The pride of the *szlachta* in being 'noble' was unparalleled – so was their pride in simply being Polish.

1 In Poland the vanity of birth is carried to a monstrous extrava-
  gance . . . If you should ask a Polander what he is he would tell
  you that he is a gentleman of Poland . . . they expect an allow-
  ance even from Heaven itself on account of birth and quality
5 [for] God would have some respect to him as a gentleman.

Although the reign of Stanislas-Augustus saw Poland being

'dragged out of the fifteenth and into the eighteenth century', the numbers of those who were directly affected by the Enlightenment must not be exaggerated. Men like the young magnate Jan Potocki, fluent in eight languages, a soldier, traveller and explorer, novelist and Poland's first serious archaeologist, as well as the first Pole to go up in a hot air ballloon (accompanied by a dog and a parrot), must always have been exceptional among the *szlachta*. The vast majority continued to believe that Poland was the best of all possible worlds, and that no deficiencies existed in the political system under which they lived. Few, if any, of the *szlachta* saw anything incongruous in a select and privileged ten per cent of the population putting individual liberty before the good of the country as a whole.

Since the early 1760s political developments in western Europe had been fully reported in Polish journals. The ideas of the Enlightenment, especially the importance of domestic reforms, were discussed by the circle of philosophers around the King. With the presence of Russian troops to back up Russian guarantees of the status quo there was, before the days of the Great *Sejm* (see page 90), no chance of putting the new ideas into practice. Critics had to be content with words, on the stage, in the *Sejm*, or in pamphlets and periodicals. All had the same message:

1 When three neighbours quietly tear away from ten million people a land rich and fertile by nature, there must be some internal cause for this . . . It is now or never that you can raise yourselves to a state of strength and decent respect, it is now or never
5 that you can ensure for yourselves the succession of the throne, for the government will be a vain illusion if the throne continues to be elective, if the king is to be a toy . . . For we ourselves are to blame for our misfortunes; we thought only of ourselves and never of our country.

By the 1780s a significant number of influential and well-informed Poles, from both noble and non-noble backgrounds, were convinced that most of Poland's difficulties had been brought about by internal weaknesses. They believed that most of the blame for the weak state of the country lay with the *szlachta* for clinging to their outmoded and unjust 'Golden Freedom'. In particular they blamed the great landed magnate families. ever feuding among themselves or exercising their right to resist, to 'the great disturbance of the people'.

c) Assessment

In assessing how far the internal weakness of Poland was responsible for the partitions, it is important to make a distinction between the first partition of 1772–3 and the later partitions of 1793–5. The situation within Poland was substantially different on the two occasions.

At the time of first partition the 'Golden Freedom' was not under any serious attack inside the country. All the political, economic and social evils which resulted from it were unabated. The King's weakness of character and the intransigence of the *szlachta* proved a fatal combination. It ensured that 'Polish Anarchy' was still alive and well. Carlyle's dictum that 'Poland was now dead or moribund and well deserved to die' being in the condition 'of a beautiful phosphorescent rot-heap', might well be applicable to 1772. It could not apply to 1793. The political scene had changed.

Many historians have made the point that the constitutional reforms of 1791, which had for so long been needed, and the lack of which had enfeebled the Republic and invited foreign interference, were themselves the signal for the death of Poland. It was not because she was weak and exhausted, and could no longer live, that Poland died. It was because she was full of new life, invigorated by political revival, that she could not be allowed to live. In the words of one author:

1 In 1772 partition had been declared imperative as the only means of saving Poland from anarchy; 20 years later, she was punished with partition for trying to set her house in order. Here was tragic mockery indeed.

It is paradoxical that, unreformed, she might have continued to survive indefinitely.

* Polish historians since the middle of the last century have mostly belonged to one of two schools of thought about the partitions. The so-called 'pessimistic' Cracow school came into being around 1860. It attacked the pervading and comfortable Polish point of view that the partitions had been entirely due to outsiders, and were not the fault of the Poles. This view had developed earlier in the century, both to assuage Polish pride and to be a direct counterblast to Prussian and other claims that the partitions *were* the fault of the Poles. The Cracow historians took the unpopular course of proposing an examination of the country's internal weaknesses in the late eighteenth century. After carrying this out, 'We had no proper government and that is the one and only cause of our collapse' was their verdict.

The 'optimistic' Warsaw school, which developed around 1900, adopted a more balanced stance. Its members stressed the cultural and economic achievements of Poland during the reign of Stanislas-Augustus. They believed that while internal weakness played a part, it was not the *only* cause of Poland's downfall. There were other, external factors involved – Poland's greedy neighbours, the balance of power and partition diplomacy.

3 The Greedy Neighbours

Any Pole who had read his or her history – available in six volumes written by Bishop Naruszewicz at the request of the King during the 1780s – would not have been surprised by the events of the late eighteenth century. They had long been prophesied. More than a century earlier in 1667, King Casimir in his farewell speech to the *Sejm* before retiring into private life, concluded by saying:

1 If your glorious Republic continues to be managed in the present
   way . . . the day will arrive and is perhaps not far off, when it
   will get torn to shreds; be stuffed in the pockets of covetous
   neighbours, Brandenburg, Muscovy [Russia] and Austria, and
5 abolished from the face of the world.

These words were echoed by Stanislas Leszczynski (see page 48) in 1734 on the occasion of his second election as King of Poland:

1 I reflect with dread upon the perils which surround us . . . We
   imagine that our neighbours are interested in our preservation
   by their mutual jealousies, a vain prejudice which deceives us, a
   ridiculous infatuation, which . . . will surely deprive us of our
5 liberty . . . Our turn will come, no doubt, and either we shall be
   the prey of some famous conqueror or the neighbouring Powers
   will combine to divide our state.

The neighbouring powers did combine to divide Poland between 1773 and 1795. (Their actions and the motives for them are discussed fully in Chapters 6 and 7; partition diplomacy is discussed in Chapter 5, pages 63–5).
  * But were the partitions inevitable? It can be argued that the First Partition was not. The Republic had survived as a Russian protectorate after the Silent *Sejm* of 1717 for over half a century. It is true that for much of this time Russian domestic affairs did not permit an expansive foreign policy, but even after the accession of Catherine II, the situation might well have remained unchanged if it had not been for the activities of Frederick II. Even then, the available evidence suggests, Catherine would have preferred to continue the protectorate rather than to partition Poland. The latter course of action may be said to have been forced upon Russia and Austria through the operation of the then near inviolable doctrine of the balance of power and its corollary, partition diplomacy.
  Did the First Partition lead inevitably to the Second and Third Partitions? The short answer is no. The rump of the Polish state remained under firm Russian control and there seemed no reason for any further partitions. That is, until the events of 1787 unwittingly brought them about. Norman Davies has constructed a 'chain of

inevitability' for the last years of the Republic. Stanislas-Augustus's well-intentioned but ill-fated attempt to negotiate an alliance with Catherine in 1787 led to the Great *Sejm* – the work of the *Sejm* led to the Constitution of 3 May 1791 – the new Constitution provoked Russia into sponsoring the Confederation of Targowica – the Confederation led to the Russo-Polish war of 1792–3 – the war led to the Second Partition of 1793 – the Second Partition led to Kosciuszko's National Rising of 1793–4 – the Rising led to the Third Partition of 1795 – the Third Partition resulted in the extinction of Poland.

 * Were the partitioning powers acting 'in accordance with the laws of self-preservation' as Bismarck and certain German historians (particularly Sybel, the apologist of Frederick II) later suggested? Against what was defence necessary? Certainly not a military threat at any time in the eighteenth century. Even before 1717 the Poles, some of the best soldiers in Europe with their famous winged cavalry, the terrifying Husaria, had only a comparatively small army on which to call. This was due largely to the unpredictable behaviour of the *szlachta* in the performance of their military obligations (see page 18). After 1717 the permitted size of the army was progressively reduced by their Russian 'protectors'. Even in 1793, at a generous estimate, the Polish army totalled no more than 40,000 men, not all of them trained. Hence the need to use the peasant scythemen in Kosciuszko's rising.

There was no possibility of Poland falling into other hands than those of her three neighbours (the Ottoman Empire was much too weak to pose any danger, and Sweden was no longer a threat). The likelihood of Poland being occupied by another and hostile power was nil. There was therefore no need to guard against this eventuality.

 * Was Poland really a potential source of revolution in eastern Europe, a hotbed of Jacobinism threatening the stability of neighbouring states in 1793? Frederick William and Catherine both declared this to be the case. Whether they actually believed it is unclear, although it is probable that Catherine did. One modern historian considers that:

1 Until the execution of the French king, Catherine could live with the French Revolution, but not for one minute with the 3 May 1791 Constitution of Poland which challenged both Russian authority in Poland and Catherine's own absolutism.

Revolution in distant France did not worry her. Finding what she considered to be similar revolutionary activities on her own doorstep was a very different matter. The reforms of the Great *Sejm* might encourage Poland to attempt to throw off the Russian yoke, and to form an alliance with her old ally, France. However, in the early 1790s, this was no more than a potential threat. A French alliance was, in any case, unlikely to be realised in view of French disapproval of the 'aristocratic basis' of the Polish revolution. The only serious danger which Poland presented at any time in the eighteenth century was that her weakness might tempt one of her three neighbours to make a unilateral gain at her expense and so upset the balance of power. Russia would certainly have been able to take over the whole country at any time after 1717 had she so desired. The fact that she did not do so was due to other factors (see page 120).

4 Reasons and Responsibility

Poland's three neighbours, Russia, Prussia and Austria were responsible for bringing about the partitions. They committed the 'crime' for reasons of national self-interest (*raison d'état*). However, conditioned as they were by eighteenth-century political thinking about the balance of power and the virtues of partition diplomacy, they would not have considered themselves to be 'villains' for doing so.

Poland's weakness was responsible for the ease with which the partitions were carried out. This weakness was military, social, economic and constitutional. The reasons for it were largely, but not solely due to the failings of the King or to the selfishness of the *szlachta*. There were other factors involved. One was geographical, although the importance of this must not be exaggerated (see page 9). Poland-Lithuania was a large country, lacking defensive frontiers and open to invasion. Largely landlocked and surrounded by her enemies, Poland was not easy to assist in time of trouble – as Walpole pointed out, 'the British navy could not sail to Warsaw'. Not only military aid was lacking. Poland had no diplomatic support either. In western Europe the will to help was absent. Poland was not only too far away and too inaccessible, but also too unknown – 'a country in the moon', according to Edmund Burke. The Poles had general sympathy – moral indignation was cheap – but could expect no practical help. In any case, whatever might be said, politicians everywhere knew that partition diplomacy had become a fact of political life by the late eighteenth century. As one modern historian puts it, 'In the eyes of Europe safeguarding Poland's independence was not worth a war.'

5 Winners and Losers

Who won and who lost by the partitions?

a) The Partitioning Powers

In 1795 Russia had acquired over 60 per cent of the total territory and population of the Republic as it had been in 1772. Prussia and Austria had divided the remaining area and population more or less equally.

As a result of these territorial acquisitions, Russia in particular increased in international standing, especially when her gains in Poland were placed alongside the substantial and unilateral ones made at the expense of the Ottoman Empire (see page 145). Russia had come of age as a Great Power.

However, the partitions were not all gain for Russia. By agreeing to partition and admitting Prussia and Austria to a share of Poland she lost her exclusive domination over the country. According to this line of reasoning, the benefits which Russia obtained by a direct rule over a part of Poland, instead of an effective overlordship of the whole country, were far outweighed by the advantages and influence which accrued also to Prussia and Austria. One historian has even gone so far as to describe the partitions as a symbol of Catherine's failure to maintain her exclusive control over Poland. In addition, the end of the Russian puppet buffer state of Poland brought the frontiers of Russia into direct contact with those of Prussia and Austria, both now substantially enlarged and potentially hostile. The Russian frontier in the west had been made vulnerable, presaging problems for the future.

The real concern for Prussia and Austria was control of Germany. Prussia needed to consolidate her scattered territories in order to pursue this policy; Austria needed to match Prussia's gains to maintain Habsburg authority. The pattern of Austro-Prussian rivalry, which was to dominate the history of Germany in the nineteenth century and absorb the energies of the two powers, was established in the partitions of Poland. Both Prussia and Austria had an equal interest in keeping Russia away from Europe. By accepting her as an ally in Poland ('the threshold over which Russia stepped into Europe' as one historian has described it), they opened the way to closer involvement by Russia in eastern European affairs, and raised up a rival to themselves there.

b) Poland

Poland as a state was the obvious loser. It could not be otherwise; as an independent country Poland no longer existed after the Third Partition.

Rousseau wrote: 'If you cannot stop your neighbours from swallowing you, at least prevent them from digesting you.' Swallowed Poland certainly was, but whether she was also digested is open to question. The Prussians melted down the Polish crown jewels, the Austrians turned royal palaces into barracks and the Russians looted anything movable. The great collection of nearly half a million books, which in 1748 had become the first public library in Europe, was packed up and sent from Warsaw to St Petersburg together with another half million volumes from other Polish libraries, to form the basis of the Russian national library.

But what about the Polish people? How did they fare? What about Polish culture and traditions?

The nobles had to produce certificates of nobility. Many were unable to do this and so lost their noble status. For most it made little practical difference to their way of life. There was little change of land ownership, for the majority of those who lost their noble status were landless anyway. However, there was a gradual annulment of the *szlachta*'s privileges everywhere, for loss of noble status meant being on a par with the peasantry in relation to liability for military service and taxation. Townspeople had to produce town charters, clergy had to register as state employees and peasants as state taxpayers. Jews who had previously been an autonomous community had to register as citizens. As they had no surnames all 800,000 of them had to be given names in order to register them. In the Austrian and Russian partitioned areas the names were usually associated with a man's place of origin, but in the Prussian area they were given names at random by the Registrar. In Warsaw the official in charge was particularly capricious:

1 Before dinner on an empty stomach, Mr. Hoffman issues serious or melancholy names, after dinner more amusing ones. In the office he sits and glares at the client in deathly silence. He then shouts the first name which comes into his head. That word
5 becomes the client's new surname. Today, being Friday, he had fish for dinner, so he has been handing out nothing but fish names – after playing the organ in church he issued names with a religious flavour . . . after drinking with a Prussian colonel military names . . . and so on.

There was no appeal against the names issued, however unsuitable they might be.

In the Russian partitioned areas an official fiction was preserved that these were the 'Recovered Territories', the ancient patrimony of Kievan Rus. A medal struck for Catherine to commemorate the Second Partition was inscribed 'I have recovered what was torn away'. Although Catherine had spoken of liberating 'those of the same faith and blood as ourselves', she did little to 'Russianise' the Recovered Territories. As R.H. Lord pointed out, her ministers and advisers wrote at length about the advantages of partition; but while there is much about strategic improvement of the frontier and about the substantial additions of land and people resulting from the partitions, there is nothing at all about Russian unity. He suggested, therefore, that it is difficult to accept the view of Russian historians that Catherine, by pursuing partition, was continuing the work of the old 'gatherers of Russian lands' and that her actions were thus justifiable. It is true that by the partition of Poland Catherine did virtually complete the political unification of Russian lands, but this appears to have been an incidental result rather than a basic cause of her policy. Even if the territory had been solidly Polish, it seems very unlikely that she would have acted any differently.

In the 'Recovered Territories', or 'Western Region', Russia introduced a centralised administration, with a network of civil and military governors. The civil service was reorganised along Russian lines and a large permanent military force was stationed in the country as a means of political control. Russian suspicions of the Poles meant that a much lesser degree of self-government was permitted than anywhere else in the Russian Empire. Despite a guarantee of religious liberty there was some persecution, most of it levelled against the Uniates. Moslems and Protestants, of whom there were few in the Recovered Territories, were largely ignored; Jews were confined to a 'Pale of Settlement', were heavily taxed, but were not otherwise disturbed. The Catholic majority suffered a reduction in civil and political liberties, their career prospects in the army or civil service were limited, the clergy were brought under state control and contact with Rome was restricted. Surprisingly, though, the Jesuits were welcomed, and encouraged to set up schools. For the peasants life became harsher as a result of increased liability for military service. It was not to change materially until serfdom was abolished in Russia more than half a century later.

Life may have been hard for most Poles under Russian control. For those under Austrian rule it was probably worse. The 20,000 square miles of Poland which fell to Austria's share became the largest, most neglected and impoverished province of the Austrian Empire. It was overseen by governors appointed from Vienna, who imposed niggling restrictions on the social and political life of the people, and introduced censorship and police surveillance. Taxation rose sharply, bringing hardship to the peasants who also found themselves liable to conscription. Serfdom also remained in force here until the mid-nineteenth century. There was little opportunity for education for anyone, and little economic or industrial development.

In Prussian-partitioned Poland conditions were better. Society was generally tolerant. Social or political advancement was not dependent on religious conformity, and Roman Catholics were not disadvantaged. Prussian control was both authoritarian and militaristic, but it was also fair, equitable and legally based. In this it compared favourably with the arbitrary and irrational government practised in Russian and Austrian Poland. Educational provision was widely available and helped the process of integration, as did the development of a thriving cultural life. The peasants were to benefit from an earlier end to serfdom than elsewhere in the region (although it was not the Prussian government itself which emancipated them). Bismarck had some grounds for reminding his critic of the advantages which Poland had received at German hands (see page 115).

The Poles could have replied that, however benevolent the occupying power may be, it is still an occupying power and its rule no substitute for national independence. There are historians who believe, despite the political ruin brought by the partitions, that in the 1790s Poland did in fact enter on a new epoch of national life, bringing with it an intensified love of country. This survived the Third Partition and gave hope to the Poles in the years which followed. The Polish national consciousness remained, even in the absence of a national state, and it became customary for Mass to conclude with a patriotic hymn, the last line of which entreated 'Restore, O Lord, our free country'. 'Anyone who feels himself a Pole, *is* a Pole' – even when there was no Poland.

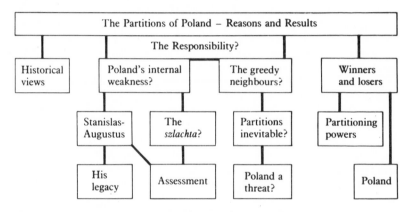

Summary – The Partitions of Poland – Reasons, Responsibilities and Results

---

Making notes on *'The Partitions of Poland: Reasons, Responsibilities and Results'*

The information contained in this chapter should enable you to present a reasoned answer to the question often asked by examiners: 'Who was responsible for the Partitions of Poland: Poland herself, or her greedy neighbours?' Keep this question in mind as you make your notes. The headings and sub-headings used in the chapter may help you.

Answering essay questions on 'The Partitions of Poland: Reasons, Responsibilities and Results'

The Partitions of Poland are a very popular choice with examiners of eighteenth-century European history, to judge by the range and number of questions set on them in recent years. It is, therefore, well worth while preparing the topic carefully. Likely questions can be grouped under three main headings:

a) Factors leading to partition
b) Poland's internal weakness
c) Who gained most from the partitions?

Within each of these groupings the questions can, and do, vary widely in scope and difficulty.

To answer any question on the Partitions you will certainly need to use information from Chapters 6, 7 and 8, and perhaps also from Chapters 2 (background information) and 5 (partition diplomacy). With so much material at your disposal you will need to be especially selective in your choice of what to include and what to leave out, particularly in any general question dealing with the Partitions as a whole. They covered a long period – more than 20 years – during which a great deal happened in and to Poland. A point to remember is that there were substantial economic and political differences between the situation in Poland at the time of the First Partition (1772) and at the time of the Second and Third Partitions (1793–5).

Occasionally you may meet a question specifically targetted on the First Partition, for example:

1. 'What factors resulted in the partition of Poland in 1772?'

But this is exceptional. Questions are usually more extensive in their coverage:

2. 'Explain the reasons for the Partitions of Poland.'
3. 'In what ways did the Great Powers benefit from the Partitions of Poland?'
4. 'Who gained most from the Partitions of Poland?'

In answering questions like these do not be tempted to lump the Partitions all together – you will need to indicate not only how conditions had changed between 1772 and 1793–5 but how this affected what happened. Sometimes the question is phrased in even more general terms, not mentioning the Partitions at all, and designed to cover all or most of the eighteenth century:

5. 'What were the aims of the Great Powers in Poland in the eighteenth century?'
6. 'Why was Russia so concerned with Poland in the eighteenth century?'
7. 'Consider the motives of the major powers for interfering in Poland between 1733 and 1795.'
8. 'Why were Russia, Prussia and Austria able to remove Poland from the map of Europe by the end of the eighteenth century?'
9. 'Why did Poland cease to exist by 1795?'
10. 'What were the causes of Polish weakness in the eighteenth century? What were its consequences?'

All these questions require what may be called 'tabulated answers' – that is, they are straightforward requests for factual information to be presented in ordered paragraphs, with an introduction and a conclusion. These 'how, why and what' questions are best dealt with by first making a list of points which you wish to include, and then deciding which is the best order in which to arrange them. Would you start with the most, or with the least important? Why? What criteria would you use in deciding your choice of order? When dates are included in the question take care to stay within the specified time span, and to cover the whole of it. Question 7 is a case in point, beginning as it does with the War of the Polish Succession and not with the First Partition.

A 'why?' question like question 6 above can be most easily answered by making a plan based on a series of statements, all starting 'because'. In this case you might include:

(i)   because Russia needed to protect her western frontier
(ii) because control of Poland would give Russia entry into Europe
(iii) because the old lands of Kiev Rus were part of Lithuania
(iv) because Poland was weak

What other reasons can you add? In order to construct your essay you need a minimum of three and ideally five or six reasons, each of which can be expanded into a full paragraph containing a range of detailed evidence to support your statement. Arrange the reasons in the order you consider most effective. Before you begin writing ask yourself why you have chosen this particular order. The essay will need an introduction and a conclusion. What would you hope to be achieving in each of these?

Question 10 is an example of the 'double', or 'two-part' type of question, which can be answered in one of two ways. You can either deal with the two parts separately, one after the other, or you can approach the question by selecting a number of aspects of the topic as 'paragraph points' so as to deal with both parts together in each paragraph. The second method is rather more difficult to carry out, but is likely to result in a more effective, because more unified, answer.

A rather different and slightly more difficult type of question begins 'how far?' or 'to what extent?'. For example:

11. 'How far were the Partitions of Poland the result of geography?'
12. 'To what extent were the Poles responsible for their own destruction?'

In each case the answer needs to be two-part one. The first part of the essay sets out reasons for saying 'This far, or to this extent, yes', while the second part looks at reasons for saying 'This far, or to this extent, no'. The essay should finish with a paragraph setting out the conclusions (i.e. the relative strengths and weaknesses of the 'yes' and 'no' arguments) to be drawn from the information you have presented.

Somewhat similar in form are questions like:

13. 'Was Poland "an island of freedom" in eastern Europe?'
14. 'Was the Third Partition inevitable after 1793?'

'Open-ended' questions of this kind can be answered in three different ways – 'Yes, because . . .', 'No, because . . .', or more often, 'On the one hand, yes, because . . . but, on the other hand, no, because . . .'.

Many questions at first sight seem complicated, especially those which are based on a quotation. For example:

15. ' "Catherine the Great was the instigator of the Partitions of which she was the chief beneficiary." Is this judgement justified?'
16. ' "The real villains were the three Eastern monarchies, not the selfish magnates nor the cowardly Stanislas-Augustus Poniatowski." Do you agree with this judgement on the Partitions of Poland?'
17. ' "It was the greed of her neighbours and not internal weakness which resulted in the Partitions of Poland." Discuss.'
18. ' "Poland – a country of little power but enormous significance in eighteenth-century European politics." Explain this paradox.'
19. ' "Poland's internal difficulties were her downfall." Consider the Partitions of Poland in this light.'

There is no reason to be put off by such questions. There is a simple technique for unlocking the meaning of such a 'challenging statement' type of question. It can be re-phrased and turned round into a number of direct questions. If this is done to question 15, it becomes: 'Was Catherine the instigator of the Partitions? Was Russia the chief beneficiary?' A second step, which may sometimes help to bring out the meaning even more clearly, is to simplify some of the words: 'Was

Catherine responsible for the Partitions? Did Russia benefit most from them?'

Once you understand what you are being asked it is a relatively straightforward matter to plan your essay. But do not forget the last part of a 'challenging statement' question – in this case asking whether it is true to say that Catherine *was* responsible for the Partitions and that Russia *did* benefit most from them. Your final paragraph should give your conclusions on these points, based on the evidence you have presented in the rest of the essay.

In question 18 the paradox – the apparent contradiction – is at once made clear if you re-word the statement as a direct question: 'Why did Poland, a weak and powerless country, play such an important part in eighteenth-century international relations?'

Re-word the remaining questions (16, 17 and 19) to make their meaning clearer.

Very often the quotation used in a 'challenging statement' suggests part of the answer, but only a part. Question 19 gives one reason for the Partitions – Poland's 'internal difficulties'. Other factors involved would need equal coverage in your answer.

Source-based questions on 'The Partitions of Poland: Reasons, Responsibilities and Results'

Read the two short extracts and Bismarck's speech on pages 114–15. Answer the following questions:

a) What assumptions are made about the Poles by the writers of the first two extracts? (4 marks)

b) To what extent does Bismarck share the opinions of the writers of the first two extracts about the Poles? Explain your answer. (3 marks)

c) How, according to Bismarck, should responsibility for the Partitions be apportioned? (3 marks)

d) In what ways have Bismarck's views been challenged by historians over the past century? (5 marks)

e) For what reasons is it unlikely that there will ever be a consensus amongst historians about the Partitions of Poland? (5 marks)

CHAPTER 9

Russia and the Ottoman Empire 1763–1800

The end of the Seven Years War in 1763 found Prussia and Austria, and to some extent Russia, exhausted, their lands ravaged and their economies under enormous strain. It is not surprising, therefore, that during the next two decades, although foreign affairs continued to be important, their rulers' attention was concentrated on domestic reform and reorganisation. However, the objective was neither peaceful nor philanthropic. It was to strengthen the state, particularly in the economic sphere, in order to support the increasingly large armies required to maintain Great Power status. In the second half of the eighteenth century this status depended on military power and the ability to use it.

One power which had not been involved in the Seven Years' War, and which indeed had enjoyed some 20 years of undisturbed peace, was the Ottoman Empire. During this time the Ottoman government had sunk back into a complacent lethargy, confident that recent military successes had restored the Empire's fortunes, and that nothing further needed to be done in the way of reform or modernisation. The long peace proved counter-productive in a state whose whole ethos had been formed by war.

1 The Northern System

In 1763 Catherine II needed a period of peace in which to establish her hold on the Russian throne and to restore the economic stability of the country. With this in mind, the minister for foreign affairs, Nikita Panin, proposed his defensive 'Northern System' of alliances. Its aims were to protect Russia's western frontier, to provide security against a possible Swedish attack, and to ensure the maintenance of Russian control over Poland. But Panin's System got no further than a triangular alliance of Russia, Prussia and Denmark – partly because of strong opposition from Frederick II. He was determined that Prussia should be Russia's only important ally.

The System in its partially achieved form remained the basis of Russian foreign policy until the late 1770s, but there was one power in the region which had been conspicuously left out of account by Panin – the Ottoman Empire. However weak militarily the Empire might in fact have been in 1763, it remained Russia's main enemy. But it was not alliance systems which decided international relations in the second half of the eighteenth century. It was the expansion of the strong at the expense of the weak, not simply by military aggression but by the development of partition diplomacy (see page 63). In the years between 1763 and 1795 the major territorial changes in eastern Europe took the form of forcible cessions of territory from Poland and from the Ottoman Empire.

2 The Russo-Ottoman War 1768–74

Russian intervention in Poland on behalf of the Orthodox Dissidents led to the formation there of the anti-Russian Confederation of Bar in 1768 (see page 75). In the guerilla-type fighting which followed a group of Orthodox Cossacks crossed the Ottoman frontier in pursuit of Polish Confederates, and caused a good deal of damage. The Ottoman government had already complained about the presence of Russian troops in Poland, and had been informed by the Russian envoy that they were being withdrawn. It was now quite clear to the Ottomans that far from being withdrawn, more and more Russian troops were arriving in Poland, many of them operating close to the Ottoman border and threatening Ottoman security. In October 1768 the Sultan issued an ultimatum demanding immediate Russian withdrawal from Poland, an end to the Russian guarantee of the Polish constitution and an end to Russian protection for the Dissidents. When the Russian envoy rejected these demands he was immediately imprisoned. War between the two countries had begun.

Neither side was ready for a war, which Frederick II unkindly described as 'a fight between the one-eyed and the blind'. The Grand Vezir had no military experience, there were supply difficulties, and failure to meet their arrears of pay had resulted in serious discipline problems among the Janissaries. The Russians were rather better organised than their enemy, although when the campaign finally began early in 1770 their army numbered only about 200,000 against the 400,000 which the Ottomans had finally gathered together.

The Ottomans started the war with several advantages. They still controlled the Crimea, which provided easy entry into Russian territory from the south; they also controlled the Black Sea, which gave them a free choice of landing and supply points along the shore for their troops; they were generally operating nearer to their base than the Russians and there was a strong possibility that they would be able to link up with the Polish Confederates. But even with their early advantages the Ottomans suffered a series of major defeats in the summer of 1770 along their border with the Ukraine, in the Danube valley and in the Crimea.

The Russian navy was also in action successfully, despite the fact that Russia's only access to the sea was in the eastern Baltic. The startling plan was for the ships to sail round Europe, calling in on the way at friendly ports for provisions and repairs, and after passing through the Straits of Gibraltar to rendezvous in the Adriatic with their new admiral, Alexei Orlov. Orlov had absolutely no experience of naval command, and seems never to have been on board ship before his appointment, but Catherine had great confidence in him. Luckily for Russia, her confidence was justified. In the meantime, plans were made to raise Orthodox peasant rebellions in Greece, intended to undermine Ottoman authority in the area and cause confusion ahead of the fleet's arrival. However, these plans proved unworkable due to a lack of peasant cooperation, and had to be abandoned. But the rest of the arrangements worked very well, and the ships arrived safely in the Mediterranean in May 1770. For the next month the Russian and Ottoman fleets chased each other around the Aegean. What followed was a repetition of the great Ottoman naval defeat at Lepanto 200 years earlier, although this time the exchange was between heavily armed sailing ships rather than lightly armed galleys. Once again the Ottoman admiral was outmanoeuvred. In a panic he withdrew with his ships into the harbour of Cheshme. At night the Russians sent in fire boats. The entire Ottoman fleet was destroyed, with the loss of 11,000 men. However, this spectacular success was not properly followed up by the Russian fleet, and an attempt to blockade the Dardanelles failed. In November the fleet left the Aegean to spend the winter at Leghorn, in north-western Italy.

The Russian campaigns of 1771 were not as dramatic as those of the previous year, partly due to an outbreak of plague which swept across southern and eastern Europe, hampering military operations there. The most important Russian success was her occupation of the Crimea during the summer. The Khan escaped to the Ottoman Empire leaving his successor to begin negotiations with Russia. These were not concluded until late the following year when a treaty was signed recognising the independence of the Crimea, proclaiming eternal friendship and alliance between Russia and the Crimea and giving Russia the right to maintain garrisons in a number of Black Sea ports, including Kerch and Yenikale. Kerch was a particularly important Russian gain as control of the Straits there would enable the flotilla, which Russia had been building in the Sea of Azov, to break out into the Black Sea.

Peace began to seem very desirable to Catherine. The war was proving a financial strain, increased taxation had led to social unrest, and the plague which had spread to Moscow in the late summer of 1771 had sparked off large-scale riots there. In addition, she was concerned about the intentions of Prussia and Austria in Poland. Already, in 1770, the Ottomans had approached Prussia and Austria with a request for joint mediation. But, when he had been told the Russian peace terms, Frederick II had refused to play any further part in the discussions on the grounds that the Russian demands were exorbitant. Catherine did not agree. She intended to hold on to what her armies had gained, and condemned the newly-coined diplomatic phrase, *equilibre d'orient* (balance of power in the east), as unrealistic and unjust in view of Russian successes.

Whatever Catherine's ambitions, neither Austria nor Prussia was prepared to see Russia make large unilateral gains at the expense of the Ottoman Empire. Austria began secret negotiations with the Ottomans for an anti-Russian alliance, by which it was agreed that the former would receive Wallachia, if she either by force of arms or by mediation secured the return of all Russian conquests to the Ottomans. News of this treaty eventually reached Catherine early in 1772. It was essential to detach Austria from this Ottoman alliance before she could declare war against Russia. This was achieved by tempting Maria-Theresa with the offer of an agreed and immediate share of Poland. From this moment the First Partition of Poland was inevitable (see page 81).

A temporary truce with the Ottoman Empire was signed by Russia at the end of May 1772. There were delays in the peace negotiations, and the situation was complicated for Catherine by the sudden threat of a northern war against Sweden, brought about by a *coup d'état* there. It was important, therefore, to prevent the resumption of hostilities in the south which might result in Russia having to fight a war on two fronts. Nevertheless, Catherine remained intransigent over her proposed peace terms:

1 On no account do I wish that the Turks should dictate to me
   what ships I may or may not have on the Black Sea. The Turks
   are beaten – it is not for them to lay down the law to us . . . As
   for Kerch and Yenikale we have not received them from the
5 Turks, we have conquered them from the Tartars, and the Tartars have ceded them to us by treaty. What need have we of
   Turkish consent?

In April 1773 the Russo-Ottoman peace talks ground to a halt. The Swedish danger had receded and Catherine accordingly felt free to consider a new campaign against the Ottomans. Plans were drawn up for a surprise attack south of the Danube. The army commander was not happy with the idea – the area was thick with Ottoman forts, and there were no maps available. He was right to have doubts about the wisdom of the plan – a Russian assault across the Danube was quite easily beaten off by the Ottoman army. Russia had suffered an unaccustomed reverse, but, notwithstanding this, plans were put in hand for a new Balkan offensive. However, before they could become operative, the situation changed with the death of the Sultan early in 1774. Direct peace talks were at once begun with his successor, but they made little progress after Catherine told him that she would not compromise on the independence of the Crimea 'even if the war lasts for another ten years'. The Ottoman side remained equally en-trenched, encouraged in its resistance by the difficulties which the Pugachev revolt had brought to Russia. (The Cossack Pugachev, representing himself to be Tsar Peter III, took advantage of social and economic unrest in 1773 to lead a peasant revolt which took Catherine two years to suppress.)

3 The Treaty of Kuchuk Kainardji 1774

Military operations were resumed in June 1774, when a Russian army crossed the Danube. It came unexpectedly upon the main Ottoman army, routed it completely and captured the camp. There could be no question this time of a truce. The Grand Vezir was given five days in which to conclude a peace treaty. The Treaty of Kuchuk Kainardji, signed in July, was a major military and diplomatic defeat for the Ottomans. By what one historian has described as 'one of the most fateful documents in Ottoman history', it was agreed that the Crimea should be independent (this left it open to eventual Russian annexation) and Russian ships would at last be granted the right of free navigation on the Black Sea. In fact, this right was not restricted to the Black Sea itself: Russian ships would be allowed to pass freely through the Dardanelles into the Mediterranean. Although these rights applied only to merchant ships, there was no limit to the number of guns which a merchant ship might carry, as one of her generals later pointed out to Catherine. Nor were there any restrictions in the treaty to prevent the construction of a battle fleet in a Russian Black Sea port, and four years later the Russians began building the new city of Kherson to be as much a naval base as a trading centre. Further clauses specified that Russia would evacuate her conquests in the Caucasus and in the Balkans. The Sultan would pay a very substantial war indemnity, and in addition would allow the building in Istanbul of 'a public church of the Greek ritual which shall always be . . . free from all coercion and outrage'. It was also agreed that the Ottoman government:

1 promises to protect constantly the Christian religion and its
  churches, and it also allows the Ministers of the Imperial Court
  of Russia to make upon all occasions representations, as well in
  favour of the new church at Istanbul, as on behalf of its officia-
5 ting ministers, promising to take such representations into due
  consideration, as being made by the confidential functionary of a
  neighbouring and sincerely friendly power.

This last article was to prove the most important of the treaty. It was so ambiguously worded that it was later interpreted by Russian diplomats as giving them the right to speak and, if necessary, to act on behalf of the Orthodox population anywhere in the Ottoman Empire. By extension, this enabled Russia, operating through the network of consuls and vice-consuls which the treaty allowed her to set up in the Ottoman Empire, to interfere in Ottoman internal affairs more or less at will, and to her own advantage, in the century which followed.

At the time, however, it was Russia's outlet to the Black Sea which seemed the most significant gain. The Austrian representative in Istanbul foresaw Russian troops being transported across the Black Sea to launch a direct attack on the city in the near future. So probable did he believe this to be that he declared, 'it was unlikely that Russia would ever again fight a land war against the Ottomans in the Balkans'. In fact, Russia did not attempt a naval assault on Istanbul for more than 100 years.

As soon as the details of the treaty became widely known in Europe, other powers, hoping to benefit from the Ottoman defeat, demanded rights of navigation on the Black Sea equal to those granted to Russia. The Ottomans were able to resist these demands, but they could not prevent Joseph II of Austria occupying the Bukovina on the northern frontier of Moldavia in September 1774 (see map on page 138).

4 The Greek Project 1780–2

The acquisition of the Bukovina merely whetted Joseph II's appetite for Ottoman territory, and in 1780 he became a willing partner in Catherine II's grandiose plans for expelling the Ottomans from Europe. Encouraged by Potemkin, her long-time lover, chief adviser and army commander, she had been toying with her 'Greek Project' for some time. It involved partitioning the Ottoman-held Balkans in such a way as to maintain the balance of power in eastern Europe (the very concept of *equilibre d'orient* she had scorned earlier), while allowing the revival of the Byzantine Empire. She justified this on the grounds that she was not only enabled, but duty bound, by the Treaty of Kuchuk Kainardji to protect the Orthodox population of the Ottoman Empire and that this was best done by 'liberating' Istanbul. The new Byzantium, based on Istanbul (formerly Constantinople), would include much of Greece. Catherine's second grandson, born in 1779, had been named Constantine, and put in the care of a Greek nurse so that he would in due course be well equipped to rule as Byzantine Emperor on behalf of Russia. Russia would also take the Balkan principalities of Wallachia and Moldavia, which would become the new and independent state of Dacia. Russian influence there would be assured by the appointment of Potemkin as the first Prince. Joseph for his part would receive the western Balkans.

The details of the scheme were worked out in a series of letters and meetings between Catherine and Joseph and presented a new and dangerous threat to the Ottoman Empire in the Balkans, which were in an unsettled state and where Ottoman control was weak. It is doubtful whether the Ottomans could have resisted a concerted attack by Russia and Austria. Fortunately for them, this magnificent scheme came to nothing. It proved impracticable – a mere pipe-dream – requiring as it did an impossible degree of cooperation by Catherine and Joseph, and an equally impossible degree of non-intervention from the other major powers. The Ottoman Empire in Europe had been saved – by default.

5 The Crimea 1783–4

The fate of the Crimea had not been settled in 1774 by the Treaty of Kuchuk Kainardji. It had merely been postponed. During 1775–6 a power struggle developed between Russian and Ottoman-sponsored contenders for the position of khan. Early in 1777 the Ottoman candidate gave up the contest, leaving the Russian one as the winner. Soon afterwards the latter, faced with a serious revolt, appealed to Catherine to send him military aid against the rebels. On hearing this, the Ottoman government at once sent assistance to the rebels. Another war between Russia and the Ottoman Empire seemed likely. The French ambassador in Istanbul pointed out forcefully to the Sultan the total unreadiness of the Ottomans for war, and advised a peaceful settlement. So, too, did Austria. Abandoned by their only possible allies, the Ottomans signed a Convention with Russia in March 1779, and recognised the Russian puppet as khan.

The Crimea remained peaceful until a further revolt broke out against the Khan in 1781. He was quickly reinstated by Russian troops under the command of Potemkin who, with others, advised Catherine to bring the problems of the Crimea to an end by annexing the territory. Catherine was not averse to recouping the expenses she had incurred in coming to the aid of the Khan, and in April 1783 she issued a manifesto proclaiming Russian annexation of the Crimea. On the same day the Khan abdicated, and retired to Russia to spend the rest of his life there on a pension granted to him by Catherine.

In Istanbul the loss of the Crimea to Russia was received with angry words, but no action. The Ottomans were in no position to go to war, bereft as they were of potential allies. France was fully occupied with war against Britain, while Austria feared that support for the Ottomans would push Russia into the arms of Prussia. In any case, there was a growing feeling among the major European powers that the Ottoman Empire was hardly worth saving. The French ambassador to Istanbul had even advised his government as early as 1770 that they should accept the partition of the Ottoman Empire as unavoidable and should take Egypt as their share of the spoils.

In December 1783 Austria abandoned any idea of support for the

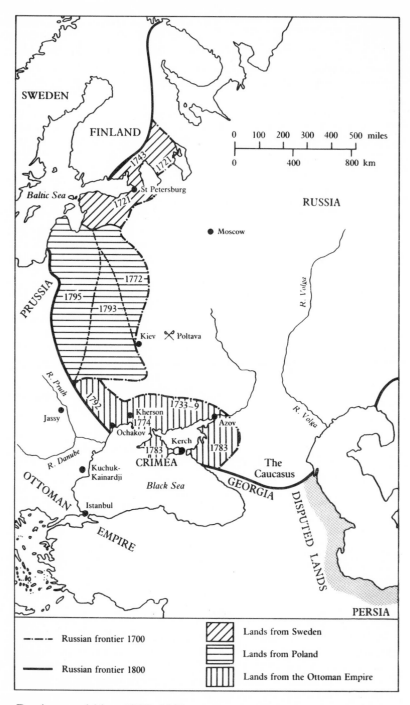

SWEDEN

FINLAND

Baltic Sea

1743

1721

1721

St Petersburg

RUSSIA

Moscow

0   100   200   300   400   500 miles

0   400   800 km

PRUSSIA

1772

1795

1793

Kiev   ✕ Poltava

R. Volga

R. Pruth

1792

Jassy

1733–9

Kherson

1774

Ochakov

Azov

R. Volga

Kerch

1783

1783

CRIMEA

The
Caucasus

GEORGIA

R. Danube

Kuchuk-
Kainardji

Black Sea

DISPUTED LANDS

OTTOMAN

Istanbul

EMPIRE

PERSIA

--·--·-- Russian frontier 1700

——— Russian frontier 1800

Lands from Sweden

Lands from Poland

Lands from the Ottoman Empire

Russian acquisitions 1700–1800

Ottomans over the Crimea and issued a declaration that, in the event of further conflict there, she would actively support Russia. Catherine commented drily, 'When the cake is baked all become hungry!' In the circumstances, the Ottomans decided to accept the inevitable. In January 1784 they formally recognised the Russian annexation of the Crimea. 18,000 square miles had been added to Russia and the balance of power in the Black Sea region was now decisively in Catherine's favour.

It was not only in the Crimea that Catherine was besting the Ottomans. In August 1783 she had signed a treaty with the most important of the petty kingdoms of Georgia, turning the little state into a Russian protectorate. Troops were sent there to build a fortress, which in due course was to become the main centre for the Russian conquest of the whole of the Caucasus. Potemkin, who had been governor-general of the Black Sea lands since 1774, took over the Crimea as well in 1785, becoming undisputed ruler on Catherine's behalf of the vast region from the River Bug to the Caspian Sea. Able, energetic and ambitious, he spared no efforts to pacify and colonise the new lands of the south, and to encourage their economic development by building roads, towns and ports. It was not long before he began to dream of extending Russian domination to neighbouring Armenia and Azerbaijan. However, his dreams would have to wait to be realised by others. The start of yet another war between Russia and the Ottoman Empire diverted his attention elsewhere.

6 The Russo-Ottoman War 1787–92

The Ottomans had become increasingly concerned over Russian expansion in the Caucasus, Russian interference in Ottoman trade with Persia, and Russian involvement in the administrative affairs of the Balkans. Accusations and recriminations by both sides merely served to raise the tension. In the summer of 1787 Catherine set out on a long-planned royal progress through Potemkin's 'fairy land' of the south. Her presence in the Crimea where she was inspecting the new naval base at Sebastopol, only a day's sailing from Istanbul, was seen by the Sultan as a deliberate provocation. When she was joined by Joseph II in Potemkin's large and splendid new city of Kherson, it seemed to the Ottomans to be a clear indication that plans for a joint attack on their empire were being made. This view was strengthened by the very large number of Russian troops gathered along the shores of the Black Sea, on which a number of recently completed and well-armed Russian ships were already sailing. If further confirmation was needed it was provided by the inscription on a large stone arch through which the royal party passed: 'This is the road to Byzantium'. It began to look to the Ottomans suspiciously like a revival of the Greek Project.

Although once again not in any way ready for a war, the Ottomans seem to have believed that they must take the initiative at once. At the end of July 1787 they presented an ultimatum to the Russian envoy in Istanbul, which he refused to accept. He was accordingly summoned to appear before the Imperial Council, the Divan, where he was presented with a demand for the return of the Crimea. Three days later he was imprisoned in the Fortress of the Seven Towers, and the war had begun. Russian war aims included the the creation of an independent state to cover the Balkan principalities of Moldavia, Wallachia and Bessarabia – more shades of the Greek Project. Joseph II was committed to aid Catherine against an Ottoman attack by the terms of an Austro-Russian defensive treaty, which he and Catherine had made in 1781 at the time of their negotiations for the Greek Project. In February 1788 he therefore entered, with some reluctance, 'a war to be fought in those accursed countries, in the midst of every disease, of plague and of hunger, and all to gain little'. Catherine too had problems. Sweden, taking advantage of Russian commitments in the south, suddenly launched an attack in July 1788 and for a while St Petersburg was in grave danger of capture. The Swedish threat eventually proved less serious than expected, but it was nevertheless a distraction to Russian efforts at the beginning of the war against the Ottomans.

The early campaigns, centred on the Crimea, were brief and inconclusive, but in 1788 Ochakov on the Black Sea surrendered to Potemkin after a six-month siege. A series of allied victories in the Balkans followed. Despite their setbacks the Ottomans, now under the leadership of a new, young and warlike Sultan, Selim III, showed no inclination to make peace.

Early in 1790 Joseph II died and was succeeded by his brother Leopold who offered an immediate armistice to the Ottomans. A year later a peace treaty was signed between the two countries, by which Austria surrendered almost all the Balkan conquests which she had made during the war. Prussia meanwhile concluded an anti-Russian offensive alliance with the Ottoman Empire, committing Prussia to declare war on Russia, to reconquer the Crimea and to guarantee its possession to the Ottomans. Soon afterwards Prussia signed a further, defensive, treaty with Poland, also aimed at Russia. Although in the end neither of these treaties was implemented, they provided a clear indication of growing Prussian unease at Russian territorial expansion, which they believed would disturb the balance of power in eastern Europe if it was allowed to continue unchecked.

In August 1790 the Russo-Swedish war had come to an end, and Catherine had begun to hope for an end to the war with the Ottomans as well. 'We have one paw out of the mud', she wrote. 'When we get the other one out – we shall sing Hallelujah!' However, although both Russia and the Ottoman Empire were tired of the war, campaigning began again in 1791. The new season started badly for the Ottomans with a series of defeats along the Danube which led the Sultan to make overtures for peace. These were very welcome to Catherine, who needed peace to be able to deal with events in Poland, where the 3 May Constitution had just been proclaimed (see page 91). After an eight-month truce, the Treaty of Jassy was signed in January 1792. Russia kept Ochakov and the land between the Bug and the Dniester rivers but returned her Balkan conquests to the Ottomans. For Catherine any 'Hallelujahs' were muted – the war might be over, but Potemkin was dead. He died shortly before the signing of the treaty which would have been his accolade as 'viceroy of the south'.

Potemkin was not the only one to have dreamt of a Russian Caucasus. In the final year of her reign, Catherine encouraged the last of her many lovers in his proposed 'Oriental Project'. This totally impossible scheme was aimed at seizing the Caucasus as well as Istanbul, so opening up the gateway to India and the Far East. His ultimate goal was a revival of the Greek empire of Alexander the Great – and more. Perhaps it was as well that Catherine died before the plan could be put into operation.

7 Russian Dominance of Eastern Europe: The Reasons?

Why in the eighteenth century were the Russians so successful and the Ottomans so unsuccessful? Was it due to Russian strength or to Ottoman weakness? Were there other reasons why, by the death of Catherine the Great, Russia had become the dominant power in eastern Europe?

a) The Ottoman Empire after 1763

The resounding defeat of the Ottomans in the war with Russia (1768–74), which culminated in the humiliating treaty of Kuchuk Kainardji, left the new sultan, Abdul Hamid, in no doubt about what he should do. Although he had spent most of his 50 years in enforced seclusion in the 'cage' before his accession in 1774, he understood clearly the need for reform if the Empire was to be saved.

Abdul Hamid was faced with enormous difficulties. During the war the already tenuous hold of central government over the provinces had collapsed altogether. Local 'notables' had acquired enormous power over large tracts of the countryside, and with their own treasuries, armies and administrations had set themselves up as independent war lords. The Ottoman sultans and their Grand Vezirs had never really understood the importance of dealing with political, social and economic problems. They preferred to ignore them and to concentrate on the needs of the army, keeping to the Ottoman *ghazi* (warrior) ideals which measured the health and strength of the state solely in terms of military glory. Abdul Hamid was no exception.

He and his Grand Vezir were remarkably successful in rebuilding and modernising the army and navy – within the limits of traditional reform (see page 00). Therefore, they introduced only the minimum of new military techniques and weapons necessary to confront the armies of Europe with some hope of success. But the Sultan went further than his predecessors in one respect. For the first time foreign advisers were not required to convert to Islam or to adopt Ottoman dress before their services could be used. This was a tentative step towards a less traditional approach to reform. The most important of these advisers was Baron de Tott, a Hungarian who had been in French service. He introduced a number of reforms into the army, but is best remembered for the Rapid-Fire Artillery Company of 250 men and officers, which he set up. These men were highly trained in his Mathematics School to use modern cannon produced in a new foundry built on the Golden Horn. The navy, too, was modernised, by an Ottoman survivor of the disaster at Cheshme, and here too the actual construction of the new fleet was carried out under the supervision of foreign advisers. By 1784 nearly 40 new ships had been completed, and some attempt had been made to improve the quality of officers and men appointed to serve in them. Efforts to improve the old Janissary and *sipahi* (cavalry) corps were less successful, due to their continued opposition to any departure from traditional procedures, but some progress was made in the introduction of new weapons and methods of training.

In theory, the Ottoman Empire ought, therefore, to have been militarily in a stronger position for war with Russia in 1787 than it had been in 1768. That this was not so was due partly to political intrigues which led to the execution of the Grand Vezir in 1785 – without his support much of the impetus for reform was lost – and partly to the death of the Sultan himself in 1789. These events left the army disorganised and leaderless, lacking in discipline and low in morale. As a result, the 1789 Ottoman campaign in the Balkans was one of the most disastrous in its history.

Peace, restored by the Treaty of Jassy in January 1792, gave Selim III the opportunity to put into practice the reforms he had been considering since his accession. A series of reports had been prepared for him on the condition of the Empire and what ought to be done. For the first time, these reports advised that military reforms on their own were not enough. What was needed was a much more comprehensive programme to include social and economic changes, for the benefit not just of the Ruling Class, but of the population as whole. But Selim, although he had for many years corresponded with Louis XVI and considered himself an 'enlightened' ruler, still clung to the old Ottoman ways. If things had gone wrong, it was simply because traditional institutions were not being properly operated. All that was needed was to rid the system of deficiencies which had developed in it, and all would be well again. He rejected the reports.

The recent war had made military failings only too apparent. Selim, therefore, began with the army. The Janissary corps was overhauled and restructured, and proper training ordered, including the use of new weapons. The *timar* system which provided the provincial *sipahis* was revitalised, and a rota system of service was introduced so that not all of them needed to go home at the same time to see to their estates. Both the Janissaries and the *sipahis* energetically and successfully resisted these reforms, and in 1794 they were still as ill-equipped for modern warfare as before.

Selim was forced to reconsider the suggestions which he had earlier rejected – clearly it was impossible to bring the traditional Ottoman forces to a level of efficiency comparable with that of European armies. Therefore, he took a revolutionary step and decided to introduce a completely new supplementary infantry force, the *Nizam-i Cedit* (the New Order), created as an entirely separate institution and financed from new sources. In this way, the New Order, organised, trained and clothed in the European manner, with European weapons and using European tactics, could be kept apart from the old corps, reducing the risk of opposition and conflict.

Alongside these developments in the army, Selim also continued the naval reforms begun in the previous reign. In addition, he encouraged the establishment of armaments factories and the setting up of technical and engineering schools based on western models. But not even he realised that European technological developments were products of the social, economic and political changes which had been going on since the Renaissance. Isolated and piecemeal military reforms of the kind he was instituting could not be successful on their own. A wider and more general programme of modernisation and change, touching all aspects of Ottoman life, was required. But the existence of this need was something no Ottoman was able to accept; problems were still best solved in the old ways. This clinging to tradition was the underlying weakness of the Ottoman Empire in the eighteenth century, as it had been in the seventeenth and was to be in the nineteenth centuries.

b) The Ottoman Empire and the French Revolution

Despite the limitations of his reforms, Selim did bring to the Ottomans a greater awareness of the west than ever before. The old isolation began, ever so slowly, to break down as a result of much freer contact between the Ruling Class and the foreign advisers and technical consultants employed in the military and naval schools. The greatest single outside influence on the Ottoman Empire after the Peace of Jassy was undoubtedly the French Revolution. Other European movements had passed the Empire by. This one did not. Selim and his colleagues believed initially that its ideals did not conflict with the teachings of Islam and that it should be welcomed; but this was largely because they did not really understand what it was about. Selim did not see in the Revolution and the death of Louis XVI any threat to the Empire or to his own absolutism – Ottoman history was littered with murders and depositions of sultans – he was simply pleased that the Revolution was stirring up discord and conflict in the rest of Europe, diverting attention away from the Ottoman Empire.

In the last years of the century the pattern of diplomatic alliances in eastern Europe was fundamentally altered – at least for the time being. After the death of Catherine the Great at the end of 1796, her son and successor, Paul I, abandoned Russia's aggressive attitude to the Ottoman Empire and began to seek some sort of alliance between the two countries based on mutual advantage. Selim was not unwilling but nothing had yet been agreed when, in July 1798, news reached Selim which caused him to change his mind about the French Revolution. The French had invaded Egypt, still nominally part of the Ottoman Empire. Bonaparte, like others before him, had decided that the Empire was not worth saving. Selim immediately broke off relations with the Ottoman's oldest ally, France, and signed an alliance with their most recent enemy, Russia, and with Britain. It was an unexpected reversal of diplomatic alignments with which to end the century.

c) Russia as a Great Power

In 1700 Russia was making her debut on the international stage; in 1800 she had graduated to a major role. Her rise to stardom began under Peter the Great. His acquisition of the Swedish provinces in the Great Northern War and the subsequent reduction of Sweden to a second-class power made Russia the dominant force in the Baltic. Peter's actions in Poland not only turned that country into a Russian satellite, but protected his western frontier and extended Russian influence into north Germany. His vast standing army, and his expanded navy, both supported by far-reaching administrative and economic reforms had proved superior to those of his neighbours. His energy and ability, combined with his exercise of absolute authority, ensured his military success. Russia was in Europe to stay.

In the difficult years immediately following Peter the Great's death,

Russia's standing in Europe was not easy to assess. Britain and France resisted admitting her to the status of major power at all. This situation changed in the middle of the century, for Russia was one of the powers which gained significantly from the Seven Years War (1756–63). Although she made no conquests, her prestige was greatly increased by victories over Prussia, and she had (until 1762) been the leading power in the coalition in the second half of the war. She could never again be ignored by the other European powers. Most historians agree that after the Seven Years War, Russia 'permanently entered the ranks of the great powers'. No other power was in a position to challenge Catherine, whose reign marked the apogee of Russian absolutism at home and of expansionism abroad (at least until modern times). Partition diplomacy found in Catherine one of its most able practitioners. With a large, well-organised army, and with both a Baltic and a Black Sea fleet, Russia was able to benefit very substantially at the expense of her weaker neighbours. Gains made in Poland were shared with Austria and Prussia, but those in the Ottoman Empire were unilateral, tipping the balance of power in eastern Europe in Russia's favour. The lands around the Black Sea were of immense strategic and economic value to her, and the port of Odessa was founded in 1794 specifically to exploit them.

Why was Russian expansion never effectively challenged during Catherine's reign? The reasons lie both inside and outside Russia. Externally, there were a number of factors working in Russia's favour. The growing rivalry between Austria and Prussia for control of Germany prevented any cooperation between them against Catherine. Colonial expansion and overseas rivalry diverted the attention of both Britain and France away from European affairs. The weakness of the Polish system of government left that country defenceless. Already under Russian control, Poland could offer little resistance. Sweden was in decline, and presented no serious threat to Russia. The inability of the Ottoman Empire to change with the times, to deal with its internal social and economic problems, or to suppress the provincial 'notables' left it extremely vulnerable to attack.

What about Russia itself? By the late eighteenth century the Russian economy was much stronger than it had been in 1763. In the last two decades of Catherine's reign the cultivation of cereals almost doubled, and the textile industry more than doubled its production. Trade generally was good, with big increases in both imports and exports. There was some industrial development, and although most factories remained small and inefficient, production of goods for the home market had reached a level which required the introduction of a protectionist tariff in the 1790s. Russia had always been sparsely populated and therefore short of labour but in the late eighteenth century the population rose sharply from 23 million at the beginning of Catherine's reign to more than 37 million by the end (the result of acquisitions in Poland, colonisation of the new lands of the south, and a substantial natural increase of population resulting from more generally settled and peaceful conditions). More labour was therefore available for use not only on the land but also in the modernised and enlarged army and navy. It was a proud Russian boast that they alone among the great powers needed no mercenaries in their armed forces. In addition, Catherine was fortunate in her army commanders – in particular Potemkin and Suvarov, who distinguished themselves in the Crimea and Poland. By their victories they brought Russia immense accretions of territory from the Baltic, the Black Sea, Poland and the Caucasus, and opened up new opportunities for trade and agriculture.

* Catherine's foreign policy was always her own. 'Be assured', she told the British ambassador some while before her accession, 'that I shall never play the King of Sweden's easy-going and feeble part, and that I shall perish or reign.' And she kept her word, as much in the direction of foreign policy as in the establishment of her 'enlightened despotism' at home. What was the driving force of her foreign policy? Historians differ in their views. One writes, 'It resulted mainly from her own lust for world renown, which successful armed aggression brought to rulers under the *ancien régime*.' Another believes that Russian wars against the Ottomans were economically motivated, 'fundamentally wars for harbours' to enable Russian grain to be shipped to western Europe via the Black Sea; while a third declares 'To the end, Catherine acted as an adventuress. Her methods remained very much the same as those which had brought her to the Russian throne'. It is arguable that Catherine paid more attention to foreign affairs than to the internal problems of Russia, because 'compared with the innumerable and insoluble domestic problems which faced her, Russian foreign policy was comparatively simple and likely to prove successful.' Expansion at the expense of her neighbours enabled her to exercise her 'boundless ambition' to extend 'her own greatness and power' and thus, as the British ambassador to St Petersburg wrote, to satisfy 'her incredible vanity'. How far she consciously pursued the greatness of Catherine, and how far the greatness of Russia, is open to question. Perhaps to her, the two were one. Certainly the most important and long lasting achievements of her reign were those resulting from her foreign policy.

However weak, disorganised and disunited her neighbours were, Russia could not have made the territorial gains which she did between 1763 and 1795 without Catherine's determination, self-confidence and driving energy, and the military power to back them. On the plinth of the great Bronze Horseman, the equestrian statue of Peter the Great which she commissioned and which stands on the

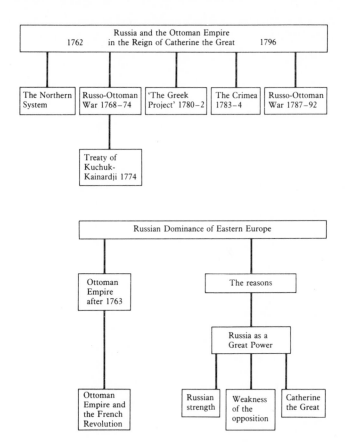

Summary – Russia and the Ottoman Empire 1763–1800

banks of the River Neva, is the inscription, 'To Peter the First: Catherine the Second: in the year 1782'. It was her claim to be regarded as his rightful successor.

***Making notes on** 'Russia and the Ottoman Empire 1763–1800'*

This chapter deals in some detail with three issues:

a) Russia's relations with the Ottoman Empire during Catherine's reign.

b)   The two wars in which the Ottomans were severely defeated.
c)   The reasons for Russian dominance in eastern Europe by 1795.

The headings and sub-headings used in the chapter should help you make effective notes which reflect this pattern of organisation.

If you began a time-chart while making your notes on Chapter 4 you will be able to complete it now.

Answering essay questions on 'Russia and the Ottoman Empire 1763–1800'

Relations between Russia and the Ottoman Empire during the reign of Catherine the Great are often included as part of a wider question dealing with Russian expansion in general. Most of these questions are straightforward, largely narrative ones, such as:

1.   'Describe and explain Russian territorial expansion during the reign of Catherine the Great.'

Again, with a great deal of material available to you, and remembering that your answer must include Catherine's activities in Poland as well as her wars against the Ottomans, you will need to be selective and to write concisely if you are to complete your answer in the time available.

Sometimes you may be faced with a rather more ambitious question:

2.   'To what extent was the expansion of Russia 1762–96 a consequence of the weakness of her neighbours?'

This 'to what extent' type of question gives one answer to why Russia was able to expand so successfully. What were the other reasons? You will need to evaluate their importance in relation to the weakness of Poland and the Ottoman Empire in the course of your answer.

Source-based questions on 'Russia and the Ottoman Empire 1763–1800'

1 The Treaty of Kuchuk-Kainardji 1774

Read the extract from the treaty on page 135. Answer the following questions:

a) Explain the 'new church' (line 4) and 'confidential functionary' (line 6). (4 marks)
b) What are the likely reasons for the Russians wanting to include such a clause in the treaty? (4 marks)
c) Why did the Ottomans look upon it as a relatively insignificant clause? (3 marks)
d) What was to be the significance of this clause of the treaty in subsequent Russo-Ottoman relations? (3 marks)
e) Explain the interest Russia had in the Ottoman Empire, other than the wish to acquire some of its territory. (6 marks)

Glossary

Russian

boyar member of the old hereditary nobility; a magnate.

dvoriane member of the newer service nobility; member of the lesser nobility.

pomestye state land held in return for service – not at first hereditary but becoming so while service continued.

votchina privately owned hereditary estate of a *boyar* family – later becoming indistinguishable from a *pomestye*, when all nobles had to serve the state.

Polish

Confederation right of nobles to band together lawfully in armed opposition to the king.

liberum veto right of a member of the *Sejm* to veto a proposal.

Pacta Conventa conditions which the king had to accept before his coronation.

Sejm representative legislative body of nobles, met every two years.

sejmik local meeting of nobles to elect deputies to the *Sejm*.

szlachta the nobility – about 10 per cent of population – very varied financial status within *szlachta*.

Ottoman

cadi judge, member of the *ulema*.

devshirme young Christian boys collected as tribute from the Balkans for service as the sultan's slaves; became obsolete by end of seventeenth century.

Divan imperial council and court of law.

kanun secular laws issued by the sultan.

reaya Moslem tax-paying subjects, usually peasants.

sipahi cavalryman.

sheriat sacred Islamic law – of extreme importance.

shi'ite fundamentalist, heretical Moslem.

sunn'ite orthodox Moslem.

vezir important government official. The Grand Vezir was the chief minister.

zimmis tax-paying non-Moslem subjects – usually peasants.

NOTE: Transcribing foreign words into English presents certain difficulties especially when the original alphabet used is different. This is true of all the words given above and of some of the place names used in the book. The usual practice is to spell the foreign word in such a way as to make its pronunciation easy for English speakers, but even so there is not always one standard English version. You may therefore find alternative and equally acceptable spellings in other books. Most differences are slight – *Krakow* or *Cracow*, *Seym* or *Sejm*, *vezir* or *vizier* – and should not give you any trouble. There is no English equivalent to the Polish letter ł (pronounced as w) and it is often treated in English as if it were in fact the letter l. Stanisław (pronounced Staniswaf) for example becomes Stanislaf, or more commonly, Stanislas. The letter j in many languages is pronounced as y. The Polish name Kollataj becomes Kollontay.

The Ottoman capital Istanbul is often wrongly referred to by western historians as Constantinople. It was renamed Istanbul after its capture by the Ottomans in 1453 and should be so called after that date.

Further Reading

There is a wealth of material available on the Russia of Peter the Great and Catherine the Great, but the years 1725–63 are not well covered in English. Most of the available information is widely scattered.

Paul Dukes, *The Making of Russian Absolutism 1613–1801* (Longman 1982).

This has a chapter on the Empresses Anna and Elizabeth, which provides a useful survey. Otherwise the book is difficult to use, being inadequately indexed.

I. de Madriaga, *Russia in the Age of Catherine the Great* (Weidenfeld and Nicolson 1981).

This comprehensive volume includes a detailed account of Catherine's foreign policy. It relies heavily on Catherine's *Memoirs* and is therefore biased in her favour. It is probably too detailed for general reading, but it is undoubtedly the best study available.

Two recommended histories of Poland which both give the reader a feel for the Polish past are:

N. Davies, *God's Playground* (Oxford 1982) in two volumes.

Volume One covers the period to 1795. This is a lively, entertaining and somewhat idiosyncratic account of Poland from earliest times.

A. Zamoyski, *The Polish Way* (John Murray 1987).

This is a cultural history of Poland, splendidly illustrated, and excellent for dipping into.

There is no entirely satisfactory account available in English for the Ottoman Empire in the eighteenth century. The following books have relevant chapters:

M.A. Cooke (ed.), *A History of the Ottoman Empire to 1730* (Cambridge 1976) Chapter 7.

S.J. and E.K. Shaw, *History of the Ottoman Empire* (Cambridge 1976) Volume One, Chapters 7 and 8.

M.S. Anderson, *The Eastern Question 1774–1923* (Macmillan 1966) Chapter 1.

Other recommended books are:

Richard Pipes, *Russia Under the Old Regime* (Penguin 1979).

Full of interesting views and information, but rather difficult to use for looking up specific points. However, it is well worth dipping into.

D. McKay and H.M. Scott, *The Rise of the Great Powers, 1648–1815* (Longman 1983).

A factual and informative political history. Far more useful than comparable chapters in general histories of the eighteenth century.

Sources on Russia, Poland and the Ottoman Empire in the Eighteenth Century

Source material on Russia for the period 1725–63 is scattered and difficult to find. There are several Russian 'Readers' available, each with a useful selection of documents in translation. One such is:

W.B. Walsh (ed), *Readings in Russian History* (Syracuse University Press 1963).

This includes, among others, lengthy extracts from the memoirs of General Manstein, prominent in the *coups* of 1730 and 1740. Catherine the Great's own *Memoirs* cover the second half of the century, but are unreliable and need to be used critically. They are available in a number of English editions.

There is little in the way of primary source material on Poland readily available in English. However, it is well worth looking for a copy of

Mickiewicz, *Pan Tadeusz* (Everyman No.842)

which, although dealing with early nineteenth-century Lithuania rather than eighteenth-century Poland, gives a splendid idea of the life of the *szlachta*.

The Ottoman Empire is even worse served than Poland and is very poorly documented in English for the eighteenth century.

1 The Ottoman Empire: Sultans of the House of Osman 1700–1800

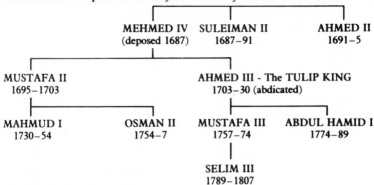

MEHMED IV
(deposed 1687)

SULEIMAN II
1687–91

AHMED II
1691–5

MUSTAFA II
1695–1703

AHMED III - The TULIP KING
1703–30 (abdicated)

MAHMUD I
1730–54

OSMAN II
1754–7

MUSTAFA III
1757–74

ABDUL HAMID I
1774–89

SELIM III
1789–1807

[Note: Brothers took precedence over
sons in the succession in the late
seventeenth and eighteenth centuries.]

2 Russia 1700–1800

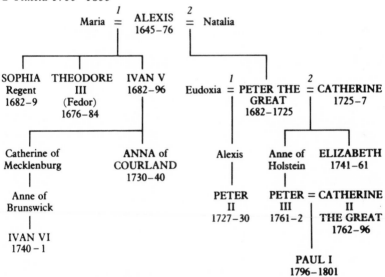

Maria $\overset{1}{=}$ ALEXIS
1645–76 $\overset{2}{=}$ Natalia

SOPHIA
Regent
1682–9

THEODORE
III
(Fedor)
1676–84

IVAN V
1682–96

Eudoxia $\overset{1}{=}$ PETER THE
GREAT
1682–1725 $\overset{2}{=}$ CATHERINE
1725–7

Catherine of
Mecklenburg

ANNA of
COURLAND
1730–40

Alexis

Anne of
Holstein

ELIZABETH
1741–61

Anne of
Brunswick

PETER
II
1727–30

PETER
III
1761–2

CATHERINE
II
THE GREAT
1762–96

IVAN VI
1740–1

PAUL I
1796–1801

3 Kings of Poland 1700–95

AUGUSTUS (Elector of Saxony) – sponsored by Russia	1696–1733
STANISLAS LESZCYNSKI – sponsored by Sweden	1706–10
AUGUSTUS III (Elector of Saxony) sponsored by Russia	1733–64
STANISLAS LESZCZYNSKI – sponsored by France	1733–39
STANISLAS-AUGUSTUS [PONIATOWSKI] – sponsored by Russia and Prussia. Last King of Poland	1764–95

Index

Augustus II 42–3, 48
Augustus III 48, 68
Azov 41, 44, 50–1
Biron, Count 27–31, 53–4
Charles XII of Sweden 42–4, 53–4
Cheshme, Battle of 133, 142
Confederation of Targowica 94–5, 100, 107
Crimea, the 49, 132–5, 137–40
Danzig 84, 99
Jassy, Treaty of 141
Kollataj, Hugo 90–1
Kosciuszko, Tadeusz 103, 105–7
Leszczynski, Stanislas 42, 48–9, 120
Nobility, Manifesto on the Freedom of 34–6
Passarowitz, Treaty of 46
Poltava, Battle of 43
Potemkin, Count 8, 93–4, 136–7, 139–41
Pruth, Treaty of the 44
Seym, Silent 48
Seym, Great 86–7, 90
Selim III 140, 142–4
Stanislas-Augustus 68–70, 82–3, 107, 115–17 *et passim*
Tulip Period 41

Acknowledgements

The publishers would like to thank the following for permission to reproduce copyright illustrations:

The Nelson Atkins Museum of Art (cover); John Massey Stewart (p. 37), The National Museum in Warsaw (p. 71), The National Museum of Cracow (p. 104), The Mansell Collection (p. 106).

They would also like to thank Longman group UK Ltd for permission to reproduce the extract from *The Making of Russian Absolution* by Paul Dukes (1988).